The First Ten Years

The First Ten Years

A Philosophical and Practical Guide to Creative
Longevity

Courtney Romano

Published in the United States by Amazon Kindle Publishing and CreateSpace.

ISBN-13: 978-0692538197
ISBN-10: 0692538194
eBook ISBN: B014KB5XSS

1. Self Help, Creativity 2. Theater, General

Printed in the United States of America.

Edited by Megan Finnegan Bungeroth
www.meganfinnegan.com

Book design by Match Zimmerman
www.matchzimmerman.com

For inquiries on speaking engagements, bulk orders and more, please visit:
www.courtneyromano.com

For Craig.

You are the invisible beginning and ending of every story I've told here.
Without you, none of this would exist.
I love you to the moon.

CONTENTS

Full Disclosure

You should know one thing before you read any further: I have no answers for you.

If you're looking for someone to tell you the exact steps to take to achieve your wildest dreams, you should put this book down.

This book isn't about knowing the right answers; it's about knowing the right questions. And there are plenty of 'em.

This book contains my answers. They won't necessarily be yours. In fact, they shouldn't be. But by honing in on the right questions, they will force you to come up with your own.

So if you want a bullet-point list showing how to make it all work, you're in the wrong place. If you're ready to ask the questions that could change your entire life, let's go figure it out.

Introduction:
MAKE
SOME
THING

The summer of my thirtieth birthday, I was on the brink of a nervous breakdown. For the past decade, I had been hustling along, living the typical life of a New York City actress. I'd audition by day and work the Day Job by night. My resume included a B.A. in Theatre and Dance, a slew of regional and Off-Broadway work, a commercial or two, and a bevy of unhelpful street cred from almost booking Broadway gigs, too many times to count. It had been a decade of getting up before 6 a.m., putting on red lipstick before 9 a.m., and dancing, singing, acting, or all of the above before lunch. I was tired.

That spring, I had been up for a dream role in one of my favorite shows and believed it was going to be my moment. Exhausted and functioning on autopilot, I went through the usual mind-motions, convincing myself that *this show would be it! This time I'd make it! My big break! My crossover into the Life I've Always Wanted! The Answer!* Then, without any fanfare, I found out I didn't get the job. It was the latest and greatest rejection in my long list of almosts. I threw my hands up. I needed to get out of town.

I'm not sure why we chose a California road trip, but for my husband Craig (who is also a creative-type, of the Actor and Photographer variety) and me, the west coast seemed the farthest away we could get from our artistic turbulence. I wanted to escape the everyday confusion I faced as a creative and was hunting down the civilian's (read: non-artist's) answers. I wanted to discover something, a nugget of insight, a new way of living that might enlighten me and give me the key to creative survival, or at least an affirmation that I wasn't a complete and utter failure. Maybe from my worn-down, pavement-pounded perspective, I thought California would be a place where Making It and Doing Something Significant With Your Life were just adorable ideas, not actual driving forces of an everyday hustle, and I wanted permission to slow down.

The First Ten Years

For whatever reason, that summer we flew to Los Angeles, hopped in our rented white Jeep Compass and scurried up the coast of California looking for the answers. We drove into the cities, the desert, the mountains, the beaches and the suburbs. For two city-lovin' New Yorkers, the variety of landscapes seemed delightfully gratuitous. The views were vast and the coast was a country in and of itself. But for all its nuanced neighborhoods and juxtaposed landscapes where I assumed Meaning and Life Lessons could potentially be hiding out, California never handed me The Answer. What I found instead were a bunch of civilians asking themselves the same questions we asked ourselves as artists. What I found were people just trying to make it.

We met a rowdy teacher who lived on a ranch and hosted travelers like us through Airbnb, a do-it-yourself bed and breakfast service that we booked online. She was rough around the edges in the way that signaled you wouldn't want to get on her bad side, but compassionate in the way that if your car broke down, whether she knew you or not, she'd open the hood. It was clear how much she loved her dogs, her ranch and her Airbnb side business. We weren't paying her much, but hosting people like us and introducing them to the coast was exciting to her. Hospitality was clearly her passion.

We met an insurance salesman who drove us around San Francisco. He sold insurance half of the week and the other half he taxied SF natives and tourists around the city in his own car. He drove for Lyft, a do-it-yourself taxi service that you booked through an app on your phone. He seemed tired and a bit road-worn, but this job was his ticket out of the traditional 9-to-5. He told us he worked every day of the week in order to support his family and get out of the insurance-selling business. Despite the long hours, he was energized. He offered us water and a phone charger. It was those "little conveniences when you're traveling that make a difference," he said. He knew what it was like after all.

We met two guys selling kettle corn. They ran what seemed to be a very lucrative business out of a truck-bed in a parking lot in Ventura Beach. Clad in tattoo sleeves and plenty of piercings, it was like buying popcorn from Motley Crue. Rock 'n' roll popcorn. Popcorn had never made us feel so badass before.

We met two young artists working in a gift shop in the Bay Area. We picked up on their vibe as soon as we walked in: it's all good. They were running this labor of love and building the cheeky handmade gifts to sell all by themselves. It seemed unlikely the store would last — even though the sassy swaddling blankets that read "Shit Just Got Real" made me laugh and I wanted one in every color — because the $43.99 price tag needed to reach a very specific, very wealthy market. We wished we could buy everything in there, but instead we had a long conversation about the gentrification of neighborhoods in SF and Brooklyn. We bemoaned the loss of the mom-and-pop culture and talked about the rent being too damn high on both coasts. In another life we probably would have been buds. At any rate, their senses of humor coupled with their attention to artistic detail made me wish an angel investor would fly in and fund them.

There were dozens of people like this on the trip we took that summer. One thing resonated with us each time we met someone new — people were figuring it out as they went. We didn't come across two stories that followed the same trajectory. The single element each person shared was their desire to create something new. Sure, there were circumstances getting in their way, but despite this, they wanted to follow their passion, leave the job they weren't excited about, grow their businesses or get their art into the hands of more people. They all wanted different tangible outcomes, but if they achieved those outcomes, the internal barometers would all read the same: success.

For creatives, this kind of living-for-the-dream-dig-your-heels-in mentality is not new. Artists in every genre have always been piecing together their incomes and their lifestyles bit by bit. They pick up on inspiration and get their hands dirty, obsessively trying to sprout it into existence. They throw their whole selves into it. They scamper around trying to promote and sell it. They do what they need to do for money, mostly just so they can get back to their creative work. They give up convention. This driving force of an artist's life has never changed.

What has changed is the rest of the world. What was once the artist's domain has suddenly become everyone's. The independence we've been granted by technology alone has made everyone a fledgling entrepreneur or amateur artist. The traditional barriers to entry, the gatekeepers and brokers and agents and bosses, have become all but unnecessary. Even funding our crazy ideas has become easier. We used to need at least one major sponsor, but now we just need to pick our favorite crowd-funding website and share a link. Some people follow this creative path because they want to make art, some because they want to make money, some want both plus a boatload of glory. Whatever our reasons, it's clear: we want to make something.

We are just beginning to understand what it means to be this new kind of creative in this new kind of world. With essentially everything at our fingertips, we can connect, share, build a platform, create a brand and self-promote to our heart's content. But somewhere along the way, all of these modern miracles start to muddy our intuition, courage and standards of success. We want Facebook likes so we pay for ads. We want followers so we follow. We buy books and go to conferences and subscribe like hell. We ask everyone else what we should do and wonder why all of a sudden we're flailing. These strategies in and of themselves are not detrimental; it's when we mix them with our need for inordinate amounts of affirmation and a lack of vigilant awareness that our dreams corrode and our days don't feel as good.

Whether it's running a bed and breakfast, a taxi service, a popcorn stand, a gift shop, or an acting career, the dream is the same: we want to "make it." And as frustrating and reductive as this is, no one else can tell us how to do that. For all the books, podcasts, interviews and magic bullet how-to lists out there, the most reliable path to "making it" is the one only we can lay out for ourselves. If we're going to spend our days making something and feeling good about it, there can be no better answer than the one we give ourselves. Our creative fortitude needs more than an app update. It needs tireless self-actualizing scrutiny. That's what this book is about.

This Is Me

No one in their right mind has ever woken up one day believing they had the answers to Life. No one has it figured out. The best we can do is evolve, and that's what I try to do. I am in the beginning/middle-ish of my lifelong evolution. You've found me at the point where I've had the right combination of existential crises and uninterrupted self-reflection to write down my experience. And what I've learned in a nutshell is this: the only way to successfully evolve (read: be okay with the utter confusion that comes from being a creative human being) is to make it up as I go. So that's what I do. I make things up and then find out if they're true.

This Is You

You are a creative. Whether you acknowledge it outwardly in the world or not, you are. You wouldn't be reading these words right now if there wasn't a distinct, small voice speaking up in your head, urging: make something. Someone may have seen this creativity in you and pointed it out enough times that you finally believed it. Or maybe you've known for a while that your advertising career was just a front and what you really want is to be a comedian. Maybe your desire to communicate large and beautiful mysteries or small and simple truths has made you stay up every night of the past year writing a new play. Or you're a freelance accountant who sees the ins and outs of finances like a complicated dance. You could be someone who works a job just to pay the bills, but sees the world in vivid color. In any case, your world is complex, your ideas are fresh, and you feel an urge to create.

But maybe when putting your ideas into practice, you've faced rejection and your battle scars have calloused over your creative pulse. Maybe too many times you haven't been able to see the bigger picture in those smallish details and you've hit a wall. You might find that you need a support system to create your life's work. Or you're lacking structure and all you need to do is define a process. Maybe you just need the permission. You could be in such a rush to create your life's work that you haven't figured out your long game yet and don't actually know what you're pursuing or why.

Whatever brought you to this moment, you're here now and the world has conspired to set your creativity in motion. Again, just to be clear, this book will not give you everything you need to build a creative life in six easy steps. You and I have both come far enough to know that this is not the way the world works. I can't guess what the answers to your particular questions will be and you should shout loudly in protest at me if I ever say I could. But I have been on the battleground, and I have resurrected my artistic life year after year, battle after battle, and so I have personal history with this moment of commitment. I have gone through the questions and doubts and flailing. I imagine I'll continue to go through them and so will you. This book is the place to write and sketch and journal and daydream and then do all those things again, year after year, as you resurrect your own creative life and find your own answers. That relentless resurgence is the moment of commitment. And if you're here, you know it's all about the moment of commitment. Everything else is secondary.

I can't tell you where you should go or who you should be or what mark you will make on the world. But I can definitively tell you this:

You have something more to give.
The world is waiting for that one thing that can only come from you.
You know how to give it.

This book is about unlocking everything that is already there, stepping into your rightful spot at the creative table, and unhinging your blocks in the name of artistic love.

So now that we've gotten that all cleared up, let's make a pact. A promise right here. To each other, and mainly to ourselves. Let's bow our heads, cross our toes, and take a vow:

To get down and dirty.
To give ourselves permission.
To relentlessly pursue kicking ass.

To free fall into the life we were meant to live, not the fabricated one we're always measuring ourselves against.
To find both abandon and order on the path to more creativity, more risk-taking and more real-world effectiveness.
To make money through these adventures, but not act as if that is the end game.
To give up the end game.
To find freedom in failure.
To live the dream instead of just chasing it.
To trust our guts.
To create communities.
To call it like we see it.
To own that we are creatives.
To settle in for the long haul.

This Is The Moment

The first time I stepped onto a bus and shipped off to an acting gig, I was 22. Just out of college. Still a baby. My dad dropped me at the bus station.

Getting the job was a whirlwind. It was late August, and I was still living at home in Pennsylvania after graduating, so I picked a few days to go into the city and audition. That first week in New York, I booked something.

I had strapped on my purple leotard and black tights (this was before those handful of years that any dancer worth her high kicks would only wear tan fishnets and lululemon to auditions) and put my full face on – red lip, heavy mascara, pink cheeks. I knew how to be the chorus girl, the understudy, the lead, the featured dancer, whatever you wanted from me, I was ready to go. You could smell it on me, the scent of cheap hairspray tinged with all-consuming desperation.

I walked into an audition for *Kiss Me, Kate* that would be performed at a theatre in Arizona. As nervous as I was *(Did I look fat? Could they tell I had no idea what I was doing? Should I have maybe fluffed up my resume a little bit?)*, when the choreographer began breaking down the sequence, I felt like I had come home. As I danced – the weight changes, the isolations, the style – it all made sense in my body. It felt good. I felt powerful. I started fantasizing about the relationship we would form. He would be like the choreographer of *A Chorus Line*, Michael Bennett, creating groundbreaking new work for his number one dancer, collaborator and actress Donna McKechnie. I would be the McKechnie to his Bennett. I would rise to stardom via regional theatre in Arizona (humility and common sense were not a part of this fantasy).

The minute the dancing was over, I slipped back into panic mode. The makeup and the movement barely covered up the looming question in the back of my head, a question that wasn't just about show business but life in general: Am I gonna make it?

The creative team thanked us for coming and said they'd be in touch. As I walked out of the studio, finally letting my perfect posture relax into tired shoulders and over-stretched hamstrings, the choreographer walked out and said, "Do you have another resume? I might have a spot open in a different show, and we start rehearsals Monday in upstate New York. Could you be there?" I nodded yes. My eyes widened. My breath stopped. He smiled and said, "I'm gonna put you to work." And with a wink he took my resume and walked away. A few hours later on my way back home to Pennsylvania, I got a call from the producer of the show upstate. In four days I needed to be on a bus to Albany. We'd rehearse for four weeks and run for four weeks. They couldn't pay me much but travel and housing were included. Was I in?

I had been expecting at least a year of struggling to even get seen at auditions, so the fact that this first gig came so suddenly shocked me into confusion. I stuttered yes.

All I had heard my whole life was that being an actor would be impossible and soul-crushing, but here I was making connections at non-equity dance calls and signing contracts in my first week of scaling the concrete jungle. Maybe this was the universe telling me I *would* "make it" one day. Maybe this was the affirmation that would carry me through the early morning auditions and streaks of getting cut and superficial jealousies of my friends that I had been told would be arriving in just a matter of time. Maybe all of those fears circling my post-graduate head were made up and this would be easy after all.

I packed up my rehearsal clothes, my LaDuca character shoes, and an opening night dress. I had heard you needed things like this as a professional actress. My dad rearranged his schedule so he could help me make my 8 a.m. bus to Albany that Monday. When he dropped me off at the Allentown bus station, he looked me in the eyes, and with a proud papa smile said, "Go get 'em kid." Without the safety net of family or school, I was legitimately on my own for the first time in 22 years. My eyes welled up with tears and I had two thoughts:

1. Public transportation makes for the most dramatic scenes.
2. This is the moment of commitment.

Up until that first gig, acting was theoretical. Making art was theoretical. I was now off to upstate New York to be in the ensemble of

The First Ten Years

Thoroughly Modern Millie, a show I hadn't even technically auditioned for. I was going to be paid $250 a week to dance in my favorite musical. I didn't know if I was actually any good. I didn't know if I'd make friends. I was definitely not clear on whether or not this was going to be my first and last gig. But maybe for all the theory I had studied and all the anxieties I had coddled and all the childhood fantasies I had nurtured, living this life would actually be okay. Maybe it'd be more than okay and fill me with the tools I needed to actually change the world, or at least be a part of it in a substantial way. I had no idea what the next decade was going to bring. I didn't realize that the moment of commitment wasn't a one-time rite of passage for a green show business baby like me, but one I'd have to meet over and over no matter how much "success" I achieved. I assumed I wouldn't have to consistently face my doubts and fears and fantasies again and again and again. I had no idea what I was beginning, but for that brief and beautiful moment, I was conscious enough to give my dad a hug, let his words fill me with courage, and acknowledge that I was about to start something huge.

This book is about that moment. It's about those moments when we decide to go left or go right. It's about the forging of all our parts into a story that carries us forward. This book is about you and your journey, and the path from well to better, the path from better to best.

It's about figuring out how to live the dream.

THE
MOMENT
OF COMMIT-
MENT

You hold the answer.

ONE:

THE THOUGHT THAT CHANGED EVERYTHING

You get that nothing's real, right? Trust me when I say I'm not writing this from any state of inebriation. As trippy as it is to consider, reality is a sham. This observation manifests when you reach a certain age, let's call it The Age of Clarity. The age is different for everybody, but the realization is the same: *all of this stuff is made up.*

"Stuff" comprises social hierarchies, and currency, and the way we organize our cities, and how we go about applying for jobs, what kind of government we have, and how we check out at the grocery store. Someone said, let's do it this way... and then they did it. Steve Jobs, the ultimate maker-upper of stuff, said:

"Everything around you that you call life was made up by people who were no smarter than you, and you can change it, you can influence it, you can build your own things that other people can use."

If Steve Jobs said it, then you know it's true.

Coming to this revelatory moment is a shock, because up until we reach it, we are fidgeting our circular selves into the square pegs of a rigid world, attempting to fit. We grew up believing we would discover our place in the world, instead of believing we would design our place in the world. There are all sorts of things that we take for granted, from the most mundane to the seemingly important, that at one time did not exist. Towering feats of modern engineering and design began as made-up notions of bold creatives. At the end of the 19th century, a young civil engineer named George Washington Gale Ferris, Jr. envisioned a massive steel structure that would lift hundreds of people into the air and spin them around in circles. Until that point, a Ferris wheel was not a thing. No one thought it could become a thing. I think we can all agree now, it's a thing. There is little you can point to in our man-made world that didn't originate from a person's brain. Nothing is inevitable until you make it so.

Before I recognized that everyone was just figuring it out as they went, I took all the things in my world for granted. I assumed there was one way of doing things and that it had been established. The mantra running in my head said, *figure out how to make all of this pre-existing life stuff work for you and for the love of God, fit in.*

Then I got older, and I started to wise up to who was actually making decisions about how auditions and governments and communities should run — people who didn't know what they were doing. Or, more accurately, people who just decided things should be a certain way, committed to it and convinced other people to agree.

I realized...

Everyone is just kind of making it up as they go.
No one holds the answer, which means everyone holds the answer.
Which means, I hold the answer.

I hold the answer.

That single thought liberated me from years (and I'm talking years) of playing small. In my world, playing small meant I didn't always go in for the important auditions for the big, Broadway shows because I thought they were "too good" for me, and I didn't connect with casting directors like their equal because I thought they were "too important" for me, and I only auditioned for musicals when I actually wanted to audition for plays because straight theatre was "too out of my league."

It also meant I kept my dreams limited to the belief that only large scale, multi-million dollar productions in midtown Manhattan were professional work. I'd go see my friends perform their original material in a Harlem church or a midtown basement theatre or a tiny warehouse in Brooklyn and think they were wasting their time. If it didn't have oodles of money and prestige behind it, according to my value system, it wasn't worth doing. Playing small gave me a narrow vision of the theatre worth producing. Playing small made me kind of arrogant.

When I first moved to New York, my Playing Small Syndrome allowed other people's ideas about the business and how to get ahead or play the game direct my own values. I had opinions, but I was respectful, dammit. I followed this self-imposed dogma that said I needed to assume others knew better in order to be a good girl.

As a newbie actor in the Land of Musical Theatre Dreams (Manhattan), I assumed the way to get a job was to audition hard and often, hold your breath, pay your dues (both to the actor's union and to the Almighty New York Theatre Gods), cry to your roommate as much as possible and then maybe one day you'd earn a tiny job that would snowball into a career as a Broadway leading lady by landing one regional theatre gig at a time. I thought auditions should be painful because everyone seemed to talk about how painful they were. I thought the only way to get a "real" acting job (once you figure out what that is, please let me know) was to have someone else give it to me. Don't tell them, but my friends who were making their own work were not doing real work in my opinion. They didn't follow the rules. They didn't book it from a horrible audition, so it didn't count.

I can't pinpoint the day I kicked that ridiculous thought pattern to the curb, because it was a slow process. It was moment after metaphorical moment. It was the quiet acknowledgement of a sentence that was whispering through my synapses when I looked around the audition room and wondered what the hell I was doing with my life. Then one day, the thought came to me like a revolution, making like Che Guevara and taking to the hills of my brain:

You know better about what you want than anyone else.

This disappointed me, of course. Following this thought would make things tricky and cause me to think critically. Just like in Intro to English, I now had to close read my life. Ugh. It was easier to go numb in my fishnets. But I couldn't shake the thought. I started decoding what I wanted to see in the world. I started to trade in my heavy, dutiful obligations for a lifestyle more reflective of my taste. I started editing my life with my own set of rules. I started feeling rebellious and energized and delighted in my work. I let my thoughts run wild with a revolution that got my brain primed to meet new people, new opportunities, new ideas.

This is all very whimsical. Here's the practical translation:

1. I started auditioning with material that was interesting to me instead of what was "appropriate" or what I thought auditors wanted to hear.
2. I didn't audition for gigs I wasn't interested in taking.
3. I stopped relating to my day job as the source of all power and security.
4. I started writing every morning.
5. I said "no" more often.
6. I looked at other people's trajectories, even ones that seemed so far out of my league, and I asked, "Do I want that?" and actually considered if it was worth having.
7. I got rid of things in my apartment that I didn't want.
8. I stopped wearing clothes that had holes in them or didn't fit me quite right.

9. I bought shoes that made me feel powerful and sexy.
10. I hung out with the friends who got me lit up and inspired.
11. I cooked at home a lot more.
12. I stopped apologizing so much.

These small acts don't seem so revolutionary to me now. Now they just feel like livin' life. But then, they were extraordinary. They released all sorts of creative pheromones into the world and I got my shit together, as it were.

This isn't a very special story. I've talked to hundreds of people who have come to the same realization. It all starts with the knowledge that we can make it all up. We can decide. Yes, bills need to be paid, but contrary to our old belief systems, there are NOT a finite number of ways to make that happen. We can really do anything we want.

As an artist, a creative, an explorer of the universe, it is your duty to define new ways of doing things. You translate for us. You build for us. You give us ideas and inspirations and evolve this planet forward into the best version of itself by holding up a mirror and saying "look." The artist takes a stab at defining existence, or exploring existence, or just deeply existing, and we need all of that juicy contemplation to open up our own channels.

So, as with everything, you need to start at the beginning. With you.

You + The World. A Love Story.

There is a whole ton of stuff in the world that can work as useful guides when going on the hunt for yourself. For instance, the things people have already made up, let's call them pre-existing systems, are great material to push against. I had a modern dance teacher in college tell us she loved ballet because she hated ballet. Ballet was a pre-existing art form that allowed her to push against it and make a whole new quality of dance based on what she didn't like. Just because we don't necessarily want to be stuck in these systems, doesn't mean they don't have something valuable to teach us. They can manifest a lot of emotionally charged responses in us, and we can use those to move forward, to figure out what we want to see.

There are five emotionally charged responses that, when elicited in us, point to our true north. They are dissatisfaction, fullness, hunger, anger, and lightness.

Dissatisfaction: This feeling comes from the systems, events, and ways of being in the world that make us feel stuck, unsatisfied and a little fidgety. Many times we feel incapable of even pinning down the feeling. Our dissatisfaction manifests in dull, existential crises at 6 o'clock in the morning. The dissatisfaction we feel is muffled by our rational mind saying: what do you have to complain about? Buck up. But whether or not we can rationalize our way out of this response, the feeling remains the same. So instead of denying it, we should take a closer look.

For me, my dissatisfaction always manifested in my bad day jobs. I always felt my priorities out of whack and for a while I was finding myself in all the wrong day jobs, being managed by all the wrong people, and fighting fighting fighting against everything. The most dissatisfaction I felt was when I was slinging beers and mixing margaritas and answering to rich men in chinos and fleece vests *Yes, you can have the salt on the rim, no I don't want to give you my number, because I'm married and wearing a starched white shirt and a tie and making mixed drinks and losing out on valuable time to be making art. Please just tip me twenty percent and MOVE ON.*

Although I was relieved to pay my rent and grateful for the opportunity to work, I nevertheless felt crappy. When I got clear on that, I was able to define what actually bothered me so I could see what I actually craved. At that job, I was dissatisfied with the way things were being led, which told me I wanted to lead. I was dissatisfied with being locked into an eight-hour shift, which told me I craved more flexibility. I was dissatisfied with being in a day job that meant nothing to me in the broader sense of being alive, which told me I needed more meaning. My dissatisfaction told me I wanted: leadership, flexibility, meaning.

Fullness: This comes from the structures that make you feel filled up, purposeful, chomping at the bit to get out there and get seen. These are the ways the world works that not only work for you, but get you motivated and move your butt to action. Feeling full isn't just responding to what is going right, but also responding to potential. The promise of more. The promise of being completely satiated by the future. Fullness is presence and potential rolled up into momentary wholeness.

Maybe for you, that's seeing a really beautifully crafted piece of theatre that gives you hope or drives you to tell your own story or reminds you of that feeling you had as a child watching something magical and spectacular unfold on stage. Or maybe what fills you up is spending a night in with good friends and good wine, discussing the universe's mysteries and telling stories about the bad old days or simply feeling comfortable in each other's presence. Or perhaps, you feel full by connecting with a child in an unexpectedly meaningful way, finding a commonality where you thought there would be none, and seeing the world through a set of tiny, fresh eyes.

The First Ten Years

Fullness is vital to creative work. You have to keep allowing your bank to fill up so you can withdraw from it. When you decide to invest in your fullness, your work will benefit. Here's the big neon sign with giant cartoon arrows and a lotta love: investment in your fullness is an investment in your creative longevity.

Anger: What gets you burning hot with anger? Don't sit in it. That's gross. Festering in it makes it alchemize into bitterness and resentment and that ain't gonna get you anywhere. But anger, when thoughtfully managed, has the power to motivate change.

I had a direct sales job selling cosmetics once. I was so entrenched in the culture and depended on by other co-workers that (I thought) quitting meant letting everyone down. I wanted to give up sales because it just didn't feel like me, but I had a team and they were looking up to me. I wanted to escape and finally, all of that bounded up, restricted, caged energy made me incredibly angry. So angry, I had to quit, even if that meant risking letting others down.

Once I quit, I learned that I had to protect my values from being manipulated. I catalogued that period of time as The Dark Year and felt immediately lighter and brighter. I realized the ties that I thought held me back were completely fictional. Quitting got me closer to where I wanted to be: I founded a theatre collective, signed with an agent, started choreographing again, got healthier. Anger got me to quit.

Hunger: This is what makes you ache for more. This comes from seeing a mode of work in the world that is already established and of which you desperately want to be a part. This is that huge exhale, shaking of the head, and saying if only... This is your insatiable-maker. Your all-consuming desire. Your most dreamy dream yet. More and more and more. That's what this is.

If you're an actor, that might mean making it to Broadway or starring in major motion pictures. You want to be seen or significant. You want a bigger slice of the action. You want coherence and connectivity and consistency in your craft. That hunger is important. I'm not saying it's everything, and I'm not saying it will ever be satisfied. But it points you in the direction of your deepest gut desire. It's the logic of your soul.

If you're hungry for something, find out all the reasons why you crave it. What about it gets you going? The size of your audience? Being able to affect a million people? The money and power that back these kinds of projects? The people working on these projects? Get clear about what exactly you're hungry for so you can find out how to feed yourself. You may not always get what you want, but this will put you in alignment with what is most truthful in your creative life. When you are aligned with that truth, there is a power that will seep out of everything you make, and that power can work wonders in the world.

Lightness: There are the systems that bring you peace, stillness, contentment. You are joyful when participating in them, you feel sustained and easy. Easiness is something we often neglect because we think hard work means payoff. News flash: It doesn't. Hard work just means hard work. I'm not saying that an overnight success doesn't have ten years of hard work behind it, but the act of doing the hard work feels easy because the act of doing comes from following your gut.

When it feels light, it is usually because it is truthful. Lies are heavy. Putting on a facade takes a lot of effort. Truth is freedom because you cut the fat. You strip yourself of the lies. Every lie is another brace we put on our would-be creatively abundant selves. Every lie is another manufactured identity, keeping the rest of us from knowing your voice and your vision.

Lightness should feel easy. Where do you feel easy? Where do you feel buoyant and energized? Maybe it turns up in your day job. Perhaps you find something you're really good at, like training other colleagues. The easiness you find there may point you to what is more interesting to you about the world. Training others might be connected to your interest in teaching, sharing, developing, inspiring. These are all ways into your craft. If you're a musician, then find a way into your craft by sharing your time with others. Coordinate a jam session. Teach a friend how to play. Read up on your favorite musician. Find the pre-existing systems that make you feel the lightest, and chances are your creative inspiration will start rearing its productive head.

Get It Down: Thoughts That Change You

What about the world dissatisfies you?

_____

_____

_____

What about the world fills you up?

_____

_____

_____

What about the world gets you angry?

_____

_____

_____

What about the world gets you hungry?

_____

_____

_____

What about the world gets you feeling light?

_____

_____

_____

What already exists that you want to affect? Change? Grow? How do you most want to relate to the world?

_____

_____

_____

Take the words that stand out most to you from answering these questions and write them down. Notice which ones are similar and which ones seem to stand on their own. Is there a common theme? An aspect that keeps popping up? Pay attention to that.

Do you see completely different themes emerging and you can't pinpoint the common ground between them? Hold onto that, too. Keep working with the words, try one on for size and see if you like it. Then try another one on until you find something that feels okay. The words that inspire you will evolve anyway.

The task is just to find out where you are now. If you can distill all of your writing down into one word, what would it be? This is your starting point. It may not be where you end up, but it's the beginning.

Choose to believe the story that moves you forward.

TWO: STARTING AND STOPPING AND STARTING

There's this thing that appears when you're about to begin a great endeavor. It all starts hitting the fan. Author Steven Pressfield, who wrote *The War of Art,* calls it resistance, researcher Brené Brown calls it gremlins, Craig calls it bullshit. Whatever you want to call it, when you're starting out, you can be sure it's going to show up.

It creeps into your creative time when you're trying to let the work flow out of you. It nestles into your quiet, in-between moments when you're trying to problem solve. It puts its feet up to stay awhile when you're sharing your work for the first time. And there's only one thing we can do to shut up this energy-sucking-willpower-reducing-Negative-Nancy-voice in the back of our heads when it's stopping us: start again.

The first time I met this voice I was eight and getting my comedic sea legs. My fourth grade class was split into groups and told to make a skit based on a Thanksgiving story we were reading. We'd each take characters from the book and expand on them to present to the rest of the class. My creative engines were revved. I was four-foot-one and on fire. I came up with this great slapstick bit where my character (the mouse) got sidetracked while giving the Thanksgiving speech, started rambling, and the other characters (including a turkey and a pilgrim) had to get me back in line. I was convinced this skit was Tony Award-winning gold. At the very least, we'd all get As!

In the middle of our rehearsal, my teacher pulled me aside. This was my moment! She was going to tell me how funny it was! She was going to say good job! I would get a proverbial (and maybe literal) gold star! But something was off - even though I knew she was about to spout unmitigated praise of my talents and intelligence, her face was pulled into an expression of disapproval.

"This skit isn't about you. You can't do it like that. It's not funny and you're stealing the spotlight."

I was mortified.

In my quiet little elementary school "I'm sorry" voice I said, "I just thought it was funny, someone else can have the part, it doesn't have to be me," but it was too late. She cut the bit.

She was my favorite teacher; I can still picture the disappointed look on her face. I loved her so much. So I believed that I had made a huge mistake by following my instincts. I believed that somehow I had hurt the other kids in my group and I was ashamed. That moment was one of the first times I learned about resistance. And as I grew up, I didn't need other people to put those words in my head. I conjured them up and listened to them in surround sound all on my own.

Adult-Made Resistance

The producer called fifteen minutes after I left the audition.

It was one of those anomaly auditions where everything was going right, but it was a long shot. I was still a non-union actor but I had watched Broadway vet after Broadway vet go in and out of the audition room to sing and dance. Then I watched them leave. And I was the last one there. I thought, maybe, *maybe* I had a shot at booking the understudy for Lois Lane in this production of *Kiss Me, Kate.*

Afterward, I hopped onto the subway to head to my catering gig, so when the producer called, it went to voicemail. In my black, non-slip, Payless shoes and leftover Audition Red lipstick, I climbed out of the depths of the subway into Manhattan's Financial District and listened to his recorded voice offer me the contract.

First I thought: *Holy shit, YES!!!*
And then immediately: *Holy shit, I can't do this.*

It was a big gig at an established theatre in Cooperstown, New York directed by a major director and paying me five times what I normally made doing regional gigs. I felt out of my league. I didn't even have my Actors' Equity card (the validation every newbie NYC actor yearned for) and I was going to be playing opposite Broadway stars. My mind started racing. This would put me in a big spotlight. I considered all the terrible things people might say about me. I tried to list them all so that I was prepared:

1. **Can't sing.**
2. **Can't act.**
3. **Can't dance.**
4. **Won't amount to anything.**
5. **This was fluke casting.**
6. **Who does she think she is?**
7. **Everyone in this show is spectacular except this nobody named Courtney.**

Despite my mental contortions twisting my confidence into a hard knot, I took the gig. Sure I was green and working with Broadway veterans, but maybe I could learn something from them that would make me a star. Sure we were going to have a 55-piece orchestra and no microphones, but I had been singing this music since I saw the Broadway revival in high school and could belt every note. Sure I was being directed by one of the biggest up-and-coming American directors, but hadn't she chosen me? One night when I was talking about it with my older brother (who happened to be an all-star football player in high school and disseminator of timeless advice thereafter) he said, "Court if you took the gig, then some part of you believes you can do it." He was right.

When we got to tech rehearsals, we added in a bit where I was to throw the bouquet to the conductor of this 55-piece orchestra. We were about to run four times a week for three months, so I now had 48 chances to accidentally toss a bouquet into a musician and bring the horns section to a screeching halt. I suppose the director could read the fear on my face as I tried a few times and failed to even get the fake plastic flowers off the stage, so she got on the microphone that amplified to the whole theatre from the front of the house to the back of the dressing rooms, lovingly referred to by theatre folk as the God Mic. "Courtney. Listen to me." The whole theatre stopped and turned to her booming, deliberate voice. "You can NOT panic. Do NOT panic. Okay? Don't. Panic."

I would have panicked if not for the ridiculous juxtaposition of her intense voice and her explicit instructions. I thought, *I'm not sure this is the way to make someone calm down.* But for a moment I recovered my sense of humor. It made me laugh and loosened me up. I tossed the bouquet to the conductor and we moved on to the finale.

Opening night was the first time I felt the phenomenon of holding an audience in the palm of my hands. It was an extraordinary feeling. I could predict what would elicit a reaction from the audience and deliver it with ease. I could move one eyebrow and they followed me. I threw the bouquet perfectly every time. And to top it off, I even got a nice mention in the *New York Times*. I felt on top of the world. What was I so worried about anyway? It was only a little song and dance show.

But then this review hit from the Canadian newspaper *The Globe and*

The First Ten Years

Mail: "How Courtney Romano got the role of Lois Lane/Bianca - in which her acting, singing, and dancing disappoints - is anybody's guess."

Yeah.

I cried for a very long time. I started signing emails to Craig (who was then my boyfriend) like this: Love, Anybody's Guess. I had prepared myself for these exact criticisms. The reviewer reached into my skull, pulled out my deepest fears, and copied them onto the page. But any amount of mental assault I had previously given myself did not prepare me for the humiliation of being publicly called out as talent-free. It hurt.

What's so funny about preparing to be destroyed is that when our Egos are completely demolished by humiliation or judgment, we will never be prepared for it. Preparing for the worst won't steel you from getting a soul beat down, you'll just end up beating yourself down for longer. Pointless.

Preparing for the worst is the other side of the procrastination coin. It's just another way of not doing the work; it's a form of resistance. Resisting the process - resisting sitting down to write, or connect, or paint, or speak, or sing, or throw the bouquet - means you are balancing on the threshold of change. You are tiptoeing down the line of almost doing and done. The energy in this spot is ripe. It's flavored with potential and fear. It's the adrenaline rush of stepping into your own skin and saying, *like it or not, here I am.* And if we can recover our sense of humor in that space, we might stand a chance of crossing over.

The energy it takes for any artist or entrepreneur to completely bare their ideas, their dreams, their vision of themselves to the rest of the world is molecular. Scientifically, you are creating neural pathways in your brain that say: *Create. Expose. Be seen. Own it.* Your brain starts hardwiring those new pathways for efficiency by turning them into habits, neurologically reinforcing the mojo that allows you to put your work into the world or at least to sit down and create it. When you simply do your work, or start it up again, or at least close the Twitter tab while you are trying to write, you are literally changing the structure of your brain to support the creative act.

On the other hand, if you choose to take your energy and repeat those nasty self-imposed mantras you've allowed in for years that say, *"No one wants to hear what you have to say. Who do you think you are? You're not smart enough, pretty enough, funny enough...,"* then your brain will start hardwiring downer neural pathways. Mojo demolished. Creativity stifled. Mantras believed.

You can choose to expend your energy creating either neural pathway, but the mission (if you're intent on being creative and unstoppable) is to follow the pathway that leads you to do the work. If you feel like you're stuck, easily frustrated, wishing you'd never started, understand this is the time to put your thing down, flip it and reverse it. Change the pathway. Set your neurological creative revolution in motion one habit-building move at a time.

Getting Comfortable with Discomfort

Discomfort is part of the journey, but relating to it doesn't have to be so messy. The difficulty rears its ugly head when we dress ourselves with the identities the world at large has prescribed for us artist-types. We don't consider what's actually true. Instead we believe:

It's so hard to make it as an actor.
You need a lot of money to have a fighting chance in a creative career.
Give up your plans of having a family if you want to be a creative.
Making art is a hobby, not a real job.
If you even get married, you'll probably end up divorced; artistic types are so selfish.
I can't stand being with another actor, we're so dramatic.
Writers are alcoholics.
Entrepreneurs are desperate.
The greatest musicians were all tortured souls.
You do better work when you're high.
You have to have a special "look" to get cast.
You can only be great at one thing, and you'll have to give up everything else.
You definitely need a Plan B.

Even if we know the fallacy in these statements, it's easy to follow the trend of believing them. When I used to tell people I was an actress, they would give me a look of absolute sympathy. *That is too bad, I'm so sorry, I'm sure you'll figure something out someday!* Was it their fault? Absolutely not. We all operate with certain assumptions until we're taught something different so when I exposed myself to whomever, I was usually apologizing for my being-an-actress-deficiency.

The day I decided to stop calling myself an *aspiring actress*, a *caterer-by-day-actress-by-night*, an *"actress"* in air quotes, I had been professionally acting for seven years, and I realized that I was, simply, an actress. No qualifiers needed. That day, I got clear about my discomfort. I thought my discomfort was with the civilian stories about a life in the theatre, but my discomfort was with saying I believed those stories when I *didn't*.

I got uncomfortable because I resisted lining up my beliefs with my actions. I resisted the stories I knew to be true:

Being on stage is about connection, and connection heals us. The theatre lets us all connect the dots for two hours.
Stability is mine when I choose it.
I have made money as an artist.
The only truly torturous thing about this career is the NOT doing it.
When I try to do other things, I'm miserable.
When I show up with a full heart, lots of good things happen.
There are enough opportunities to go around.
I'm okay with the things I can't control.
Artists are some of the most compassionate, intelligent people I know.
Being in the flow of work is better than any drug.
There is enough love to go around for your spouse, your kids, your career.
My need to create is bigger than my need to control.

If you want to make a life as a creative of any type, you have to choose the stories you believe and don't believe. These are the stories that will help you move past resistance. When you build your habits, each time the bad review hits, the gremlins start getting louder, or the civilians pity you, you have another chance to reinforce the real story. You have another chance to habitualize truth and ritualize the alignment of your beliefs and your actions. Habits are the antidote to giving up. Willpower and logic will get you there initially, but for the long haul, your habits determine your success.

Get it Down: Comfortable Discomfort

What are some hyperbolic statements you've heard or said about your craft?

_____

_____

_____

Who do those statements serve?

_____

_____

_____

What is the opposite of each of those statements? Do the opposites hold any truth for you?

_____

_____

_____

What do you get out of actually participating in your craft? In writing, acting, building your business?

_____

_____

_____

How would you describe your craft to the lay person who has never heard of it before? How does it benefit the world?

_____

_____

_____

Notice any overlaps from the last worksheet. Can you start to see where your passion and purpose intersect? Any similar phrases or keywords that stand out? Use these as cornerstones in conversations about what you do.

The practical details
exist so that
we can keep
coming back
to our
work.

THREE: SPACE, MONEY, TIME

When you tell your friends about your latest project writing and starring in a hip, new web series about the annihilation of the rainforest and how to turn around the destruction of the earth, they might have questions. The questions won't stop at what *Where did you come up with that?* or *Have you done this before?* They'll also want to know how you do it: *Does that pay? Do you need a day job? Where do you live? How do you find the time to do everything you do?* The fact that you might be sick of these questions, that these questions will force you to engage in massive amounts of self-control to keep from rolling your eyes, doesn't make them any less valid. You should be asking yourself the same questions. We can avoid talking practical details and act like they don't matter, or we can own that this is a realistic part of the artist's life.

But before diving into practicality, let's get clear with what that practicality is ultimately serving. The constraints of space, money, and time are all real dimensions to our work, but we need to think of them like bumpers. We slam into them from time to time only to get back onto the path of art-making and dream-pursuing. They are not the measure of our success, but they are the steady comrade keeping us in line. Our work can't happen without them. The practical details exist only so that we keep coming back to the center of ourselves.

Space, Taking Your Stage

Actors have stages. Painters have studios. Writers have desks. Well, at least in a perfect world they do. In our ideal artistic settings, we have all the space we need to create our masterpieces. We have enough quiet to think, enough stimulation to focus, and enough room to move. In a perfect world, we live without lack. But in this very real, very loud world, we have to get uber-specific in setting up our workspace.

When we do this, we are signaling a shift to our brains. We step into our artist dome and rev up for some down and dirty creating. At one point in my career, I didn't step onto the stage for three years and it's no big surprise that those were the years I was living in a 400-square-foot apartment full of clutter I just didn't need. Have you seen *Hoarders*?

You get the point.

Many times, we buy into the notion of spatial scarcity and use it as an excuse to do nothing. This happens frequently in big cities like New York where you can't even take your daily subway commute without spooning a stranger. But scarcity is an idea just as much as abundance is an idea. We choose to see what we choose to see.

The question comes down to this: how much space do you really practically need to get to work? For all the times I've bemoaned my cramped city-living, there have been an equal number of times I have created dances in my kitchen, written on my bed, sung in my bathroom, rehearsed sides in my living room, on the street, in an elevator...

The point is, we don't need much space to just start. As our work grows, sure we'll want to carve out a little more room or rent a studio for a couple of bucks, but we don't need a grand rehearsal hall or writer's retreat *to get started*. All we have to do is be willing to take our stage, own the space we *do* have, and get to work.

Spatial Relevance

Spatial relevance is a way of looking at your world that magically transforms scarcity into abundance. To create this, we have to infuse our spaces with enough order and stimulation to allow our minds and bodies to free the hell up. We have to repurpose our spaces to accommodate the fullness of our imaginations. This means cleaning off your kitchen table, or making your bed, or painting your walls. It means working in another room far away from your roommate, or taking a seat at the coffee shop, or blasting your music. For me, if I want to clear my space to write, I do three things: clear off my desk, light a candle, turn on my writing music. This makes my space feel vast. My creative waves start to flow.

By completing those three simple rituals, my tiny one-bedroom apartment doubles in my mind. Even when Craig comes through the door and suddenly there are two of us taking up space, it still feels expanded because of my intention to expand it. I focus. I write.

Transforming your space from scarce to abundant is about getting clear with what drives you and what holds you back. It's about being honest about the environment you need to do your best work and then going about the task of creating that with whatever is at your fingertips. Spatial relevance assumes you can write your masterpiece in any space, as long as you claim it.

And how much we claim the space is proportionate to how much we believe we deserve.

We take up as much or as little as we're willing to comfortably occupy. We expand and contract depending on how much of our honesty we are willing to let out. It's important to remember: letting ourselves take up more space doesn't crowd it out for anyone else. Contrary to popular belief, as we expand and take bigger and bigger pieces of the pie, the pie expands. There is always enough space to go around, there is always a place to practice, sing, dance, write, act – but you have to step into it. You have to declare your intention to get to work, and then you have to do it. The space will expand on your command. When you commit, the resources appear.

Money, The Day Job Complex

Let's hit everyone's favorite topic, shall we? It takes money to create. It just does. And I'm not just talking about creating the work; in order to create the *possibility* for the work to actually happen (read: pay the rent, groceries, bills, basic human needs) we need the green. We can get all touchy-feely-hopey-changey about finding our joy and discovering our true nature and yadda yadda yadda, but the bottom line is: we gotta get paid.

So there are a few ways creatives tend to handle this conundrum.

1. We get bitter about the Day Job.
2. We make the Day Job our savior.
3. We use the Day Job as an excuse.

Bitterness + The Day Job

This is your tried and true route to resentment, fatigue, and all-around nastiness. For many artists in big cities, this bitterness approach is attached to working in a restaurant. It was for me at least. For the first few years in New York, I catered, waited tables, tended bar, made a lot of money, didn't have to do too much heavy lifting, and was for the most part in a stable financial position. Oh, and I had health insurance. Naturally, I was miserable.

To be fair, my restaurant manager was a micro-managing, leering, faux-paternalistic creep of the highest order. His interests included chiding his staff for placing the incorrect quantity of foam on the cappuccinos, offering wholly unwelcome life advice, and not taking the blame for his own mistakes. And he had a disturbing fascination with my marriage.

Craig and I had been married for less than a year when he booked an out of town gig for nine months. He was performing at a prestigious Shakespeare festival but not making a lot of dough, so I was busy picking up extra shifts at the restaurant. It was the best of times, it was the worst of times.

One Friday during happy hour, I was muddling mint and sugar in a furious attempt to make seven mojitos for the chino-wearing, fleece vest-clad men from Credit Suisse when my manager pulled me off the bar to have a talk. I thought for sure I had sent out sub-par cappuccino foam and was about to get reamed out. After all, what other reason would be important enough to pull away from muddling duty at 5 p.m. on a Friday night?

We walked to the little out-cove where we normally held pre-shift meetings. It was the place where our delightful manager would check our uniforms, and if there were any stains on our long white aprons or the degree of our shirt sleeves' starched crease wasn't sufficient or a single hair had fallen out of place (the worst offense of all), we could be sent home for the night. I checked my hair in a passing reflection. *Did I miss a flyaway?*, I thought.

We entered the out-cove and he sat on a bench. I stared at him, waiting.

"Go ahead, have a seat," he said. I sat.

"Courtney, how are you? Everything okay?" he asked.

"Yeah, everything's good," I answered.

"How's your marriage?"

I shifted uncomfortably under my starched, rigid uniform as I wondered what the hell he was doing. "It's great. He's away right now working at a regional theatre, which is tough, but I'm going to visit him soon."

"You just," he sighed, looking for the right words, "you just seem sad. You haven't seemed yourself. How long is he gone for?"

"Until May."

"Oof. So you have about five more months that he's gone. You've been here quite a lot."

"Yeah, it's a really prestigious gig, but it doesn't pay as much as he made here, so I'm just working extra shifts is all," my voice got quieter and more suspicious with every word.

"You're an actress, too, right?"

"Yep."

"Ya know, I don't get it. You're very smart, very talented, why don't you do something else? You could do anything."

"I agree, I am smart and I could do anything. And I choose to be an artist," I answered.

"What if you were a director, or something that paid more and was more prestigious?" he offered.

"I'm not interested in that right now, and none of it really pays well," I let him know.

He laughed. "You should have married for money."

"I married for love," I said without laughing.

"Well I just want you to know that I'm here for you. I know things are tough right now between you two. Trust me, I know marriage is tough even when you're in the same city, so I know how hard this must be on you. Just know you can come to me whenever you need."

"Thanks," I swallowed my anger, "I think a big group just walked in, I should get back."

"Yep, go back out there," he put his hand out for me to shake. As if we had just made a deal. As if we had connected. As if I wasn't crawling out of my skin. I shook his hand and scuttled back to the bar, never happier to mix mojitos and keep my head down. I knew what that therapy session was all about. It was a test to see how far he could go, how willing I might be. It was such a cliché, which somehow made it worse.

That interaction, among many more, made me exquisitely bitter. I was plain old angry and I couldn't snap out of it. Was this the Day Job's fault? Nope. Was this even creepy manager's fault? Nope. The job itself was so secure, so lucrative that I hooked my mind around the idea that without it I would never make money again, I'd lose our apartment and Craig would be forced to quit his huge acting opportunity in Alabama because I just couldn't hack it alone in New York. I couldn't imagine the unknown that would come along with quitting that job. So instead, *I became exquisitely bitter because I judged my success by how much or how little I needed the job.*

My idea of success was based on stability. Stability is a fine thing to want, but like I said in the first chapter, when I'm being honest I don't actually crave stability. In terms of what I value and desire, stability comes way after vibrancy, unpredictability and lightness.

Practically, the job was a great resource for me, but without it *I would have just found another job.* My mistake was in thinking there was no other way to make enough money, so the things that bothered me about the job became heavier, more dramatic, and certainly took up more of my focus. The illusion of stability kept me chained to the job longer than necessary. I felt stuck. And stuck is not the same as stable.

Savior Complex + The Day Job

While I couldn't leave the bartending gig quite yet, it didn't stop me from relentlessly looking around for the next magic bullet that would save my sorry butt. And remember how I told you that I was putting anxiety out into the world and getting back loads of disappointment? I was also putting desperation out into the world and getting back everyone else's equation of happiness because I wasn't defining what I wanted.

I was searching for anything, *anything*, to get me out of this bitterness state to which I had immigrated. I wanted a different Day Job, but not just that, I wanted *a good one*. When I started out in New York, I used to say that finding the perfect Day Job was like finding the perfect ex-boyfriend; it couldn't be done. But as the years of working for tips piled on, and despite knowing I had never found the perfect ex-boyfriend, I became obsessed. Now, it was my mission to disprove my own theory. I *had* to find the perfect Day Job.

I hadn't worked on a production for a while (shocking, I know, considering how I was always holding hands with my buddies Righteous Anger and Desperate Longing) and I figured that since I was never going to be a successful working actress again, I might as well be a successful second-rate something that would actually make me money. So in an attempt to find that magic bullet, I took a direct sales job selling cosmetics. I liked makeup; they said I'd make money. In my state of obsessive desperation that all sounded like a plan. It didn't matter that I wasn't passionate about sales; I would pretend. It didn't matter that selling made me feel a little slimy; I would hop right into denial. Because all I wanted was to feel *good at something.* I wanted a win and would indiscriminately accept it from anywhere.

The stakes were high. I was a validation addict. A gold star junkie. Every Tuesday, I booked a ZipCar and drove to a conference room in a New Jersey hotel to get my affirmation fix. I'd walk into the beige, carpeted, airless room and plaster on the slightly-too-large smile everyone else was wearing. Dressed in some sort of skirt or dress, which was required, my heels would sink into the carpet and I'd find myself waddling toward the desk where I paid my dollar to get in.

"The dollar is to cover the cost of ribbons," the nice, smiley, somewhat creepy lady told me at one of my first meetings.

And man, did we get ribbons. At the first ribbon ceremony I attended, I watched a woman with a microphone rile up the crowd by reciting a long, seemingly endless list of names and numbers:

"Jenny Lee Good Girl, $200 in sales!" The crowd cheered and Jenny Lee ran up to get her ribbon. Sprinted, really.
"Fiona You Deserve An A+, $375 in sales!" Bigger cheers, faster running.
"Tammy You Are Worthy Because You Followed Directions, $925 in sales!" The crowd jumped to their feet as Tammy took a slow and deliberate walk to claim her prize. A red ribbon with the number $925 on it.

The first time I saw this, I thought. *Ribbons? Really?* But despite my instinctual aversion to polyester flaps of fabric with numbers signifying how much cleanser I sold each week, something about a room full of women cheering each other on was such a stark contrast to being isolated and interrogated by my skeevy manager. The ribbons and cheering and skipping to the front of the room became appealing. Not to mention, my good girl complex was in high gear and my inner competitor secretly coveted a ribbon. And not just any ribbon, the *best* ribbon.

This show of success was highly intoxicating. It felt like The Way Out. Except, the show of success was just a show. It turned out that I was only seen as far as what I could do for those above me and only valued at how much profit I could turn. Nowhere in the history of my life had I been more obsessed with making money, even though none of it aligned with my joy. None of it brought me closer to my authenticity. None of it made me feel successful. If anything, fighting against all this inner turmoil, this soap opera of phantom success, brought me further and further away from feeling good.

The job wasn't a bumper. It was everything to me. It consumed me. It exhausted me because I was doing something that didn't align with my priorities. I allowed other people to influence my priorities because I wasn't setting boundaries. I believed this was my last stop out of town and if I couldn't make this work (read: be the most successful, make the most money, have the most influence) then I was destined to be a bitter out-of-work actress for the rest of my life instead of what this job could make me if I did it right: a *successful* out-of-work actress for the rest of my life. The job was flawed, the bigger picture was flawed; I wasn't moving forward.

Excuses + The Day Job

This might be the most prevalent combination of our anxieties outwitting our dreams. The art of the excuse. I have mastered this, my friends. I can come up with a list of reasons as to why I am completely unable to go after what I want. Usually it has to do with "responsibilities."

One of the best kinds of Day Jobs you can have as an artist is one where your time is flexible. You decide your hours and you can schedule around auditions, your writing schedule, your gallery opening, your shoot day. But with great power (to schedule) comes great responsibility (to resist over-scheduling). I have been known to schedule myself with Day Job work so tightly that the possibility I'll have any energy left to show up and sing my face off is a joke. I have been known to cite *they need me* as an excuse to work during the exact time I should be at an audition. Like I said before, needing money is a real thing. I'm not saying we don't *need* to make money to survive, but how easily do we twist that to block us from doing what we came here to do? How easily do we use it as our reasoning out of the tough task of creating? We pretend like we don't have time or energy or space because of the Day Job but none of those obstacles are insurmountable. We can figure it the hell out. We can get to (real) work. We can excuse ourselves forever, but if at the end of the day we haven't made what we wanted to make, then why are we doing the Day Job anyway? The Day Job isn't the excuse. It is the how.

The Alternate Reality

So there's one more option for relating to your Day Job. And let's get one thing straight before we dive in: *most artists have Day Jobs*. Even the most revered artists give big speeches or teach a course from time to time. Sure, those are artistically fulfilling to some extent, but let's be honest, they are Day Jobs. Their point is to bring in the green. So let's demystify our relationship to these bad boys and get really clear about what it means to have a Day Job:

1. Having a Day Job is a fact, not a failure. Let's stop believing that the less we need the Day Job the more successful we are as creatives. Let's stop judging our success as creatives by anything other than the contentment we get out of creating our art. If you still haven't bought into the idea that Day Jobs are merely facts, take a look at the Day Jobs of these very famous, very successful, very creative artists:

Taxi driver: Philip Glass reportedly loved the independence driving taxis granted him. He kept it up until his music paid more of the rent than the driving.

Used bookstore clerk: Jasper Johns worked in a bookstore to support his living in New York when he first arrived.

Insurance company worker: Franz Kafka complained about how much time he had to devote to his Day Job and yet somehow churned out masterpieces like *Metamorphosis* despite what he saw as an inconvenient schedule.

Bookstore clerk: Vincent Van Gogh also didn't enjoy his Day Job, but he found the time to doodle and translate passages of the Bible into English, French and German to pass the time.

Teacher: Mark Rothko taught at Brooklyn College even as he became more famous and sold more paintings, becoming a household name.

Graphic designer: Andy Warhol drew advertisements for magazines as he gained his own unique style and stardom.

Farmer: Robert Frost worked on a farm for nine years. The farm that ended up in his most famous poems.

Public relations: Kurt Vonnegut worked in PR as a technical writer. But this didn't stop him from writing in and out of work hours.

Poorly paid governess: Charlotte Bronte worked for a few families in Yorkshire. One summer, one of the children she watched allegedly threw a Bible at her. Some speculate it could have been the inspiration for the opening of *Jane Eyre* when, coincidentally, John Reed throws a book at Jane.

2. Having a Day Job you dislike is temporary. There are plenty of fish in the Craig's List sea. Open up your mind and realize that you are working one job out of a million other possibilities. Sure, it might take some pounding of the pavement, but if you are really that unhappy, it's your mission to change it. Your creative work will not wait for the perfect Day Job. Your work needs to come out. The only way you can steer it into the light is to maintain the light. When your Day Job gets so tedious that your creative light starts dimming, head for the hills. I promise that the hills have more job opportunities than you think.

3. Having a Day Job you enjoy does not mean you should abandon your art. When the stars align and you are in a steady job that is right up your alley, chances are you're going to believe you have to abandon your artistic passion. The saying goes, "if you CAN do something else, do it!" Right?

The First Ten Years

That was the thought in my head after I finished teaching one of my first group fitness classes. It was a good class, I had a good group, the right words were finally coming out of my mouth. Everything flowed. It was fun and I was energized. I had cracked the code and found a job that stimulated me. Then as I was putting the weights away, I thought, *am I a fitness instructor? I thought I was an actress.* I believed this unhelpful lie that actors could only ever be good at acting, so now standing in the middle of the studio, sweat dripping from my forehead, Aasics double-laced, and endorphins on overdrive, I thought *Shit, I'm going to have to quit show business.*

There are plenty of people who find something else that lights their fire and subsequently change directions, but I wasn't experiencing that. You know the difference: it's not when you'd rather throw your entire being toward a completely different calling, it's when you're finding that you're good at more than one thing. If you are a creative of any kind, chances are you're going to be good at multiple things. You spend your days problem solving and seeing from different perspectives. So yes, that's going to mean we get good at a variety of skills. Enjoy your job, enjoy what you do to make money, then let it bump you back to work so you can make new things. Both can exist. It's not a competition.

We have this crazy identity complex when it comes to working a Day Job for money and working a passion for love. We think they are separate, but the truth is, everything is interchangeable. Sometimes love makes us money, sometimes money turns into love. Whatever your Day Job is, you are still a creative. You are who you are whether you are awake to it or not.

Why Your Day Job Bothers You So Much

If despite knowing all the facts about Day Jobs and gaining a realistic perspective about what it takes to make art you still feel unsatisfied with your Day Job, it's not about the job. You are unsatisfied because you can't see the bigger picture. I repeat: it's not about the job. It's about your vision, your direction and your goals. You don't know where you're going or why you're headed there. Your foresight is muddied and because that isn't clear, the reason you are making money in this particular way isn't clear.

When we know our ultimate purpose, our why, our bigger significance, we can identify what needs to get done. This purpose gives meaning to a job that is meaningless. You have to get clear about where you're headed to get clear about where you are.

When that makes sense, a Day Job easily fits into the master plan.

Time, Minding the Gap

Along with having the space and money to get to work, you also obviously need the time. Again, we work with scarcity here: *I won't have enough time to practice, I won't be ready in time, I really need more time with the material, it's not ready yet, it needs more time before I can share it.*

When you sit down to work every day, you always have enough time. Your mind gets primed and ready to activate. Your creative synapses are itching to fire because you are creating a habit. At first, to the overworked and under-rested, that might sound like fantasy. I'm not suggesting you're not swamped with the never-ending deluge of work emails, or that you're not carting your kids around between their seven different after-school activities or that you're not working three jobs just to keep the heat on. What I *am* suggesting is that to get into your creative space and unlock your flow, all you need to do is take one simple action.

One action, repeated daily, will help you build a habit so that creativity can wiggle its way into your world without you even knowing it. That one action will build the habit that makes working on your craft as natural as everything else you do. Not sure what that one action should be for you? Try one of these:

Under Five Minutes
1. Free write for five minutes and see what your mind comes up with. Ask yourself this question to get started: What is the next step in my process?
2. Practice sensory overload. Attempt to notice every sight, smell, sound and texture around you. Practicing taking information in will help reinforce your ability to slow down and make space for inspiration.
3. Capitalize on your commute. Pick one small task that will push you forward in your process and make it a point to complete that task during your commute, waiting in line or in those small moments of downtime at work.

Under 20 Minutes
1. Meditate for ten minutes, then free write for ten minutes. Clearing your head and giving yourself room to process will light up inspiration.
2. Use your lunch break. If you work 9-5, let your lunch break be your time to work.
3. Show up early. When making plans with friends, show up twenty minutes before anyone else to get some of your ideas rolling.

Under Five Hours

1. Allot your time and don't get up until you've met it. Close your tabs. Turn off the Internet. Work until the buzzer goes off. But for the love of all things holy, commit to getting your ass in the seat.

In many cases, we waste time thinking we're working when we're really not. So what do you define as real work: trolling social media or writing the next great American novel? That was the tough-love question Craig asked me when in a tearful, exasperated fit I cried to him, "I just don't have enough time to get all of this done. I have to write for my work blog, and my own blog, and my friend's blog, and those other blogs I'm doing for free. Why am I doing those for free again?! And I have to edit the next chapter of my book. And prep for my day of work tomorrow. And we have no groceries so I'm going to resign myself to being hungry and pissed and unable to do anything useful at all because I JUST CAN'T!"

God love him, at that point in our marriage, he had seen one of these over-worked, under-rested nervous breakdowns a few too many times to co-sign my bullshit.

He said, "Courtney. You have more time than you think."
"No I don't," I cried. Literally, I was crying.
"Tell me what you've done so far today," he said in his calmest, most practical tone. This was the tone he used to get me out of deep shit if I would just listen.
"Well, I mean... I had to do a lot of research on building a platform. Because ya know, if I want a literary agent, ya know... I have to have a platform. So I had to figure out what a platform was and then figure out how to build it and ya know, I don't have time to build a platform! I have to keep liking things and following people and I don't even know if it's

paying off…"
He cut me off, "That's not your work. Right now, your work isn't building a platform. Right now, your work is writing. You have enough time. You're filling it with everything but your work."
"But… I'm… But…" I had nothing. I sighed. As per usual, his logical, loving conclusion was right. I wasn't actually doing the work that I was hoping people would follow. I was avoiding it.

Most of time scarcity is based on the fear of actually showing up to the page, or stage, or canvas. We have the time, we just don't have the courage. And the only reason we don't have the courage is because we think we are showing up to do our best work and we're scared that we can't do that. Listen. Sometimes we can, but the other 95 percent of the time, we're showing up to just do *something*. We back down due to space, money and time scarcity when what is really frightening us is a lack of worthiness in our work. We think, *what if it's no good and so it's just not worth the effort it takes?* Our job is not to judge whether or not our work is worthy; our one and only job is to make something.

Ira Glass, master storyteller and famous host of the podcast *This American Life*, put it best. Memorize this if you can:

"Nobody tells this to people who are beginners, I wish someone had told me. All of us who do creative work, we get into it because we have good taste. But there is this gap. For the first couple years you make stuff, it's just not that good. It's trying to be good, it has potential, but it's not. But your taste, the thing that got you into the game, is still killer. And your taste is why your work disappoints you. A lot of people never get past this phase; they quit. Most people I know who do interesting, creative work went through years of this. We know our work doesn't have this special thing that we want it to have. We all go through this. And if you are just starting out or you are still in this phase, you gotta

know that it's normal and the most important things you can do is do a lot of work. Put yourself on a deadline, so that every week you finish one piece. It's only by going through a volume of work that you will close that gap, and your work will be as good as your ambitions. And I took longer to figure out how to do this than anyone I've ever met. It's gonna take a while. It's normal to take awhile. You just gotta fight your way through."

Become the Freelancer You Are

The best thing I ever learned how to do was freelance for myself. I had been signing 1099s and working independently for a decade of my life, but I was always linking myself to the company handing me the 1099s. I was a cog in the machine of the theatre industry or the Day Job or even in the commercial idea of being an artist. When I found much more time to do my work (the work I found stimulating and purposeful), I found that I had reduced my loyalties to machines and recommitted loyalty to myself. Myself, Inc.

At one point, I was so intent on working just as hard for myself as I did for others that I made a spreadsheet and clocked in my hours.

Rehearsing monologues: 1 hour
Vocalizing, learning new sheet music: 1 hour
Scouring the web for auditions: 30 minutes
Writing a few new scenes in my play: 2 hours
Editing the next chapter of my book: 1 hour

I even put a pay scale key in the spreadsheet so I could see how much I would be making if this were for someone else. I think I theoretically paid myself a whopping $10/hour. I was valuing the no-one's-ever-gonna-see-this-but-it's-integral-to-my-success work I was doing by a dollar amount. It was completely out of touch. The whole point of those hours was to foster something deeper in my work, not to continue clocking in and clocking out. Working for myself was supposed to feel different, but I was approaching my craft like I had been approaching my other jobs. I operated under the make-believe assumption that putting in hours follows a straight line to payment. It was all so linear and logical. Except, being a creative is anything but linear and logical. Needless to say, the spreadsheet didn't keep me focused. It just pointed out that even *I* wasn't going to give myself a living wage for reciting monologues.

Then one day I was talking with a co-worker, the kind of person who you meet and just *get*. Her aura was always contemplative. Her pace was always thoughtful. She opened me up every time I talked to her. I walked into the fitness studio where I was about to teach four hours of back-to-back classes feeling exhausted, and she read it on my face. She said, "What's up? What's going on?"
"I'm just tired."
She smiled.
This made me smile.
She said, "If you worked as hard for you as you work for others, you could do anything you wanted to do. I have no doubt in that."

My super guru soul sister highlighted the fact that, for creatives, stepping up to the plate of our potential starts by giving ourselves permission to jump all in.

Jumping in and owning the fact that we are freelancing then opens up a whole world of possibilities. Hustling through a Day Job, creating time wealth, and fostering spatial abundance is all part of becoming your own boss. It's how you lay down the serious sweat you need to stay focused and on top of your non-linear, colorful, albeit chaotic, lifestyle. Hiring ourselves, giving ourselves permission to hurdle forward into the unknown with unadulterated enthusiasm, is the most essential element to our success.

Get It Down: Define Your Borders

What stimulates or inspires you the most? Colors? Scents? Sounds? Maybe your most creative space reminds you of your summer vacation as a child or instills a sense of urgency. Figure out the specifics. Do you need coffee, loud music, timers, or a clear, simple uninterrupted space? Start with your senses and stimulate them in the way that makes you feel the most open.

_____

_____

_____

_____

_____

_____

Define your larger purpose. What does money buy you? What does time buy you? Is it comfort? More freedom? Adventure? On a scale of 1-10 write how much you need that one thing? Is money the only way to attain it?

How can you access the end goal of comfort, freedom, adventure, etc. now?

_____

_____

_____

_____

_____

Do you schedule your creative work like everything else that's part of your day? Do you give your creative time as much value as you give your money-making time? What are you doing that is pointless - that doesn't actually serve your overall purpose? How long does that take? Do you spend two hours nightly wading through emails - could you replace that time with writing, singing, creating?

_____

_____

_____

_____

_____

_____

DOING YOUR WORK

The end result
of your
process
is in
direct relation
to how much you
own
your process.

FOUR:
THE
VOICES IN
YOUR
HEAD

Everybody's a critic. When you're a creative, people feel free to share those criticisms with you. Creativity is subjective after all. Outside opinions can be helpful when you're swimming around in your own thoughts for too long, ideas shriveling up like prunes and losing their density. One of the fastest ways to master our craft and re-energize our long games is to absorb feedback and implement strategic adjustments along the way. We are malleable, fluid beings and our power lies in our ability to interpret an ever-changing world. But interpreting criticism to make better work means sifting out the productive kind of feedback from the worthless kind. And there is plenty of worthless feedback out there.

I have created some hard and fast rules for myself when I'm on the front end of any process. When my work is at the earliest stage of creation, I get all mama bear and protect my art baby so it's essence doesn't get distorted by unnecessary opinions. I make it a point to dismiss:

- those who offer criticism without offering their own vulnerabilities.
- people who tell me what my process should be.
- feedback that tears the bigger project down while I am still building it up.
- too many well meaning high-fives.

Expose Yourself, Please

First off, if you're not offering your own vulnerability it probably means you aren't on the battlefield. And if you're not on the battlefield, the truth is, you don't have a very good vantage point. Yes, it's crucial for creatives to get that outside eye, but if it comes from someone who has no idea what it's like to be in the trenches, what good is it when we're in the trenches? We don't need help with the finished product. We need to fortify ourselves down there in the mud and shit. I am much more interested in those who have gone before me, or who are fighting next to me or have at least been through enough battles that their advice isn't theoretical. They have the scars to prove their case. They have been wounded and gotten back into the pit and tried again and so they can share what worked for them. Their criticism sounds more like solution-based ways forward, rather than the negative observations of those Debbie Downers who dislike just to dislike.

When we become so enamored with criticism, feedback, or affirmation from outside sources who haven't earned our trust, we are throwing our guns, ammo, and fireballs of instinct away. We're surrendering. Our power goes out the window. But we don't have to give up power. Our instincts are enough. We recognize this every time we see a child at play. The kid operates from instinct. She's not looking around for affirmation. *The way I'm swinging on this swing-set, jumping off of it, and hurling myself across the soccer field - it's okay, right?* You don't go hurling yourself across the blacktop because it has been critically reasoned. You do it because you can't contain your excitement.

The same with art, my playground buddies. Our instincts are there, but we block them as we let more and more chatter in from the outside. We shut down our senses every time we let someone in who doesn't belong in our creative space. This loss of power will deplete every ounce of energy in your bones. It will deflate your instinctual spirit and dry up your creative flow. You'll end up worn out. You'll say, *Never mind guys. That tire swing looks great, but I think it's safer for me to just go inside and watch what you're doing instead.*

When the giver has not offered their own exposure, whether by doing the work you're doing, having a history with this kind of work, or offering their own vulnerabilities in some other way, ignore the feedback. Dear Creative Being, please take this particular advice especially to heart. Love, Anybody's Guess.

Theodore Roosevelt nailed this:

"It is not the critic who counts; not the man who points out how the strong man stumbles, or where the doer of deeds could have done them better. The credit belongs to the man who is actually in the arena, whose face is marred by dust and sweat and blood; who strives valiantly; who errs, who comes short again and again, because there is no effort without error and shortcoming; but who does actually strive to do the deeds; who knows great enthusiasms, the great devotions; who spends himself in a worthy cause; who at the best knows in the end the triumph of high achievement, and who at the worst, if he fails, at least fails while daring greatly..."

The dust and sweat and blood guy, now *he's* got something we can all use.

Process This

One of the most thrilling things you can do as a creative is acknowledge your own process and not be afraid to use it. In undergraduate acting class, you learn a lot about different methods and teachers, what others believed to be the best way to develop a scene. But there is an indelible mental shift on the day you decide what works for *you*. It seems simple enough, but it's actually a very deliberate act. You begin to follow an inner voice that says, *go this way.* You might not know why yet, but you know which road you need to follow. To watch yourself in your craft and then make adjustments is, I believe, one of the keys to longevity.

I was originating the lead role in a new play about an Italian mob family and a week into rehearsals I got the unhelpful kind of feedback - the kind that makes its way to your ears but wasn't intended for you to hear. A cast mate said something along the lines of, "She's not making any choices. She's boring."

At first I mentally catalogued all the smart-ass comebacks I would use the next time I saw him. *Who the hell are you? I was working hard! Didn't I get cast in this role for reason? I don't need you to be bullying me behind my back and also you're an idiot who doesn't know nothin' about nothin'!*

But then I wondered if he was right.

Turns out he was. I was boring. I wasn't committing to anything yet. Not because I wouldn't commit, but because I was at the front end of my process. I knew that if I went too far down the stereotype road, I'd end up imitating the Italian mob princess archetype and my character would lose her edge. I knew if I played up the accent right away, I'd lose the meaning of the words. I knew if I went for the obvious bigger-than-life physical choices, I'd miss the undercurrent that would motivate my body to naturally move like this woman. I wanted it to be organic and I couldn't be interesting until I understood her. Even if everyone else understood her surface level, I couldn't dress her up until I knew what she looked like naked. It's a method of character development called working "inside-out."

Some actors work the opposite way. They start with bold choices and edit from there. They always impress me. Being in a rehearsal with them is exciting. You never know what brilliance they're going to pull out next. As an actor finding my way through a new piece, I love working with those kinds of artists. It keeps things shaky, and behind closed rehearsal doors that's all kinds of fun. Sometimes I wish I was that actor, but that's just not me. When I build a new character, I have to work methodically. I piece her together from the bottom up so that she feels second nature. I was externally boring because it was the internal stage of my process.

First we learn to speak, and then we learn to sing. We are constantly evolving and our process should, too. When someone criticizes your process while you are in the middle of it, if you listen to their criticism, you lose that essential soul element that steers your ship. You lose the ability to decipher what your body and feelings are telling you. The process becomes about pleasing someone else instead of finding the truest, most direct route to storytelling that you can find. Your process will be constantly in flux, so you need to protect your ears in order for your intuition to be your guide.

If I had let his criticism seep in, maybe my cast mate would have liked my performance better, but I would have made a meaningless, stale outline of my character and been a huge disappointment to myself. The end result of your process is in direct relation to how much you own your process. Criticism of *how* you proceed will not make your end result stronger, it will only make your work less your own.

Building It All Up

A lot of this particular rehearsal process was spent ducking out of the way from this actor's useless kind of criticism, which hurdled in my direction almost every day. It was just one of those shows. Sometimes the vibe is all kinds of lovely, sometimes it's fatalistic. I had to avoid the crashes of negativity and criticism aiming for my head all through rehearsals and tech.

Tech is the day or two a production gets to transfer the work they did in the rehearsal hall to the stage. It's where we add lights, costumes, entrance cues, set pieces, quick changes, music cues, cut scenes, add scenes. Essentially, it's where the show goes to die and be reborn. When we make the transition from rehearsal hall to stage, everything falls apart and tech is the process of putting it back together as fast as possible before an audience gets in the seats.

One night during this tech process, waiting in the wings to enter for the next scene, I heard my critical actor friend whisper under his breath, "Oh God, this show is going to kill my career." Then we entered stage left to try and piece the next scene back together. Would the show be brilliant? Maybe not. But in order to at least *try* to make something meaningful happen in that scene, I had to block the voice of the guy who wanted to tear down the entire project before we had even finished building it back up.

We have all been part of a project that has been a challenge. We have all been in work environments that felt less than professional. So what?

The idea of value, in terms of art-making, gets tossed around a lot, but nobody really seems to agree on what it means. Some people think a project has value if it has financial success. Some people think a project's value has to do with the celebrity or known names associated with it. Some people think value has to do with a smooth ride, everything working out perfectly and not getting into trouble during the creative process. For my money, value depends on connection. Will the audience leave the theatre or gallery or exhibition or lecture or website having something to talk about, good or bad? After all, unless we're completely self-indulgent, isn't our creative impulse nudging us toward discovering and knowing and understanding each other at the most basic level? Don't we look at pieces of art and, in the best-case scenario say, *"Hey I recognize that. I feel less alone."*?

When we work with other artists who define value differently than us, letting those attitudes, as understandable as they may be in less than ideal circumstances, invade our own heads completely misses the point. You either choose to build or to destroy. You will either make it better or make it worse, and it's your decision how it will all go down. No, there are some pieces you can't save. There are some lines that don't make sense. There are some moments that will fall flat. It doesn't matter. It is your job as an artist to rise above the challenge and force the work to be elevated, even if it's just an inch. It is your power to decide whether or not to be taken seriously. It is your fault and your fault alone if you can't stand in your work. No matter what is said, you have to do the best you can do. Tearing down the project because it has a million and one odds against it won't make you succeed even if it fails. It'll trap you in inevitable failure without having learned anything in the process. It's a supreme waste of time.

Too Many Well Meaning High-Fives

On the other side of the criticism spectrum, there are the bullshitters. The people you ask for input because you know they'll love anything you do. I delight in asking these people for feedback on my work. The good girl part of me, the little lady who seeks insane amounts of affirmation and treats it like scripture, loves loves loves the bullshitters.

I play the part of the bullshitter for myself from time to time. Usually it happens when I'm focused on how I look and not the work itself. But here's the thing about making better work and, as Ira Glass puts it, closing the gap between your good taste and your good work: you have to seek out being the worst one in the room.

You have to seek out sucking.

When I was in college, I majored in Theatre and Dance. I had already been studying every form of dance for my entire life. I was pretty good. But I never took an advanced dance class in college. Well, that's an exaggeration. I took one advanced class one semester to work with a guest teacher who was only teaching advanced classes. But other than that, I stayed at the intermediate level. None of my friends or advisors quite understood why. I was the lead dancer in many dance concerts. I had featured roles and dance solos from the moment I was a freshman. My fear of sucking kept me from taking those advanced classes. In retrospect, keeping myself safe at that intermediate level was a terrible waste of time. Instead of making myself the worst one in the room, I learned to be great at being mediocre. I didn't want to fall. I wanted to land every turn. I wanted to be the best even though what my dancing could have used was a little willingness to be the worst.

It's the only way to get better. In any room you're in, you have to want be the weakling, the least qualified, the least experienced. It means you're open to absorbing the strength, qualifications and wisdom from those around you. It means you're about to gain something you didn't already have. That's where our work starts changing. When it's not good enough yet is when we push ourselves to make it better.

Bullshitters are great. Don't get me wrong, they make me feel so good. But now, the people who can tell me something I don't know yet, who help me see in a way I haven't considered yet are the people I want to be around the most.

Who We Let In

Even though I'm a strong believer in protecting our vulnerability from those who mishandle it, I am also deeply committed to the idea that our work cannot grow and morph into its fullest potential without outside air. When I started writing, I realized I needed to write a piece and share it with the world to see if it was truly what I wanted to say. Creating something all alone, sheltered away from everyone definitely forms a magical sphere of comfort. You imagine everyone is pickin' up what you're layin' down. You might even think you have communicated just what you wanted to say. But I believe you have to let your work see the light of day to understand its essence.

The act of putting your work out there for the world to digest allows you to handle it with more insight, compassion, and nuance. When we release our precious art babies to others, we have to see them the way others see them and then, being the good parents we are, we bring them back inside the house, clean them up, and send them out again. It is a process of exposure and editing and rebirth. It is how we find out what we believe, and when we find out what we believe, we will do whatever it takes to communicate it.

Sharing your work is integral to growing your work. There was a point in time when I didn't want to put anything on social media for fear of being judged or laughed at (I had no proof anyone would do this, my inner demons were just loud and proud). Since I have committed to being as acute with my truth-telling as possible, I look at social media as a shrewd ally for honesty. There are plenty of people who feel telling the truth is much less entertaining than their twelfth selfie of the day with another photo of their food. Or those whose life looks like a magazine shoot, who surely don't need to work because people must offer them money just to continue being so awesome. But when used like a truth-tellin' boss, social media connects your work to the people who need to see it and unlocks some major power.

Presenting bits and pieces of your work online makes you...

- Accessible to everyone and anyone.
- Vulnerable, and therefore, provocative. And provocativeness equals power to hold attention. And attention means a further-reaching voice.
- Trust that there is space for your work.
- Give permission to everyone else who is afraid to share their work.
- Relevant.

What if we treated our online communities like visionary communes instead of insecurity dumping grounds? Then we might all just sink our teeth into our true and raw potential: that spark of excitement that splits into a courageous attempt that morphs into a new conceptualization that forms itself into some really worthwhile Work.

It's worth considering that if we wholeheartedly commit to not only making our work, but sharing it with others, that self-promotion might turn into an *actual* promotion. Elevating us to the next level. Connecting the dots where before were only impossible gaps. Creating a buzz around our unique vision in order to not just look ahead at what our work could be some day, but to the present moment and to what our work looks like right now. Our flawed and imperfect and useful work.

Can we just make a pact? Can we flood each other's inboxes and newsfeeds with good, real, raw, creative, amateurish-gonna-be-something-someday work that defines who we are and this moment we exist in? Can we burn up our anxieties with the practice of exposure?

The First Ten Years

Can we just find our voices and let 'er rip?

Get It Down: The Inside Outside Critic

What is the worst criticism you've ever gotten?

_____

_____

_____

What is the best feedback you've ever received?

_____

_____

_____

Did you believe either?

        Yes   **No**   **It's Complicated**

Explain:

_____

_____

_____

_____

_____

_____

What's a piece of feedback you consistently give yourself? What feedback do you always give?

_____

_____

_____

Do you apply it to your own work?

_____

_____

_____

How can you take the right kind of feedback and filter it into your work and your process now?

_____

_____

_____

Your work cannot make a *real* **impact** if you don't **know** who **you** are.

FIVE:
ARRIVING
AT THE
PARTY

In college, my favorite acting professor used to tell us that when we go to an audition we need to *change the energy in the room*. For a 21-year old whose biggest relationship with energy up to that point was figuring out how to muster up enough of it to kick her leg high in Intermediate Ballet after a night of playing King's Cup, I didn't quite understand what she meant. My professor explained that we couldn't change the energy in the room until we believed we were invited to the party. What she meant was, in the audition room, everyone wants you to be The One, but you can't be The One until you're willing to believe in yourself. Believing in yourself is one of the most cliché things people tell you about pursuing success in the arts, so let me be specific.

Believing in yourself means you believe in your ability to do the work.

You merely show up to be seen and you don't really care what happens next. That source of your belief, that thing that allows you to simply show up to be seen, has a prerequisite: confident vulnerability.

Confident Vulnerability

So my 21-year old self didn't quite understand how to change the energy in the room because I was young and fearless. When I was growing up in dance class, my mentor always told us to be fearless. "Fearless dancing! Don't dance small!" Couple that with having a football coach for a father and the president of the teachers' union for a mother, and you get the childhood mantra of: *Go for it!* Not a bad mantra to inherit, but I was missing something. To really effect change, my fearlessness couldn't completely displace vulnerability. They had to co-exist. Tempering that fearlessness with vulnerability was harder than I thought.

Early in my career, I showed up to present my auditors with exactly what they wanted to see. I sang the right notes, gave the right line readings, and you better believe I was impeccably dressed for the part. I thought this was fearlessness. I thought the act of being in front of people who were going to outright judge you was "going for it." And don't get me wrong, when the hundreds of actors I see every day and I show up at auditions to stand in a small room and attempt to create some magic in under two minutes, we all believe we are going for it. But there are moments when the energy crackles in that audition room and there are moments where the energy stifles with sameness. The latter is what happens when you're fearless enough to show up, but you don't allow any part of yourself to be vulnerable when you do.

So What Happens Now?

I was fresh out of college and auditioning for the non-union tour of *Evita*. I had the perfect song ("Someone Else's Story" from *Chess)*, the perfect dress (red, of course), and the perfect look for the Argentina-based musical (you know, Italian). Perfect. I had been waiting for a few hours when they finally called my number and lined us up in the hallway to audition. As I stood there, thinking about how prepared and perfect I was and what it would be like to go on my first national tour, I overheard the girl in front of me in line talking to the monitor. The monitor was telling her, "Oh you are so perfect for the mistress. What song are you singing?" The girl in front of me said, "'Someone Else's Story' from *Chess*." The monitor said, "Great, that is a perfect song. I will drop a good word for you when I go in. You would be so good in this role."

Panic and sweat poured out of my skin. I had prepared. I had the right song. I thought *I* was perfect for the part and now I had to follow up someone else and why did I have to overhear that conversation and it wasn't fair! After quelling my panic attack, I thought I'd make a strategic move and change my song to "Another Suitcase in Another Hall." It was from the show itself, it was sung by the character I wanted to perform and I felt like I had to play offense. Okay, I could do this. It would be fine. I had sung this song a hundred times. I just had to be fearless and go for it.

The girl ahead of me sounded good. *Dammit*, I thought. As she walked out, I gave her a meek and fake *"You sounded greaaaaaat"* smile and took a deep breath. Then I stepped into the audition room and all hell broke loose. I started singing my new song and words escaped me. I stood in the center of the room for what felt like hours as the pianist kept playing but no lyrics came out of my mouth. There stood perfectly presented little me, half-smiling, eyes glazed over, waiting for the only phrase of the song that I could actually remember, which was, I kid you not, "So what happens now?"

I couldn't believe what a train wreck I had created. I was prepared, why did I have to change songs at the last minute? It was because I didn't allow myself to be judged against someone I assumed was better and more qualified for the part. If I had sung the same song, maybe they still would have chosen someone else, but they would have been able to see my confident vulnerability instead of my fear and insecurities.

I decided I was down, but not out. They were having a dance call the next day, so I packed up my LaDuca heels and my swallowed pride and tried again. I thought maybe they would forget what I did the day before, love my dancing and give me a second chance to sing. Confident and vulnerable, in I went.

We learned the combination faster than usual. There were maybe 17 high kicks, 75 triple pirouettes, and what they call in the biz, a cooter slam. Maybe some of that is an exaggeration, but we did have to end the combination with a triple turn into a split. I knew I could do it, but I also knew technique wouldn't be enough. I had to prove I was a capable performer. I threw myself into the difficult choreography and the emotional story behind it. I even grunted my way through the tough parts. It wasn't necessarily beautiful, but it was real. It was raw. I showed up. And I was cut.

Shooting for perfection led me to failing, but failing is what teaches us who we are. I had had the worst audition of my life, came back fighting for it, still lost, but two things happened: it gave me a great story for parties and I realized it felt much better to be cut the second day when I had really shown up and been seen without trying so hard to look perfect. That knowledge sustained me every time I walked into an audition after that. At least I could fall and still get back up. At least I knew I was willing to be messy and get out of my own perfectionistic way. I finally realized, you cannot step into the party and shift the energy of the room if you don't know who you are.

When I put on all the right clothes and (sort of) sang the right songs and smiled at the right time, I was dampening my vulnerability. As Brené Brown says, I was putting on the shield of perfectionism. I wasn't exposing myself, I was presenting an idea. And while I was displaying fearlessness, I lacked the real confidence of letting myself be exposed. Brown really distills this the best:

"The word persona is the Greek term for "stage mask." In my work masks and armor are perfect metaphors for how we protect ourselves from the discomfort of vulnerability. Masks make us feel safer even when they become suffocating. Armor makes us feel stronger even when we grow weary from dragging the extra weight around. The irony

is that when we're standing across from someone who is hidden or shielded by masks and armor, we feel frustrated and disconnected. That's the paradox here: **Vulnerability is the last thing I want you to see in me, but the first thing I look for in you."**

Vulnerability is the courage to be fully seen.

Confident vulnerability is the trust that when you are finally seen, even if you don't get the part, you are enough.

Why No One Likes a Perfectionist

Still not convinced to let the armor tumble down? Well, I'm writing this with all due respect, but no one wants you to show up to the party as your most perfect self. No one ever looks at someone else's story and is inspired by how perfectly they lived their lives. Think about this. Those who inspire you the most, the stories that get you all sorts of lit up, the moments which move you to action are usually about overcoming. I have never heard anyone say, "I'm so inspired by how everything fell into place for her and how normal that seems to be in her world. Woohoo!"

As a Recovering Perfectionist, I can tell you with great sincerity:

We don't want perfectionists at the party because...

- They are always tired, exhausted by their own willpower to succeed, succeed, succeed!
- They have impossibly high standards that no one can relax around.
- They get defensive when faced with new ideas.

- They get defensive when trying to troubleshoot a problem.
- They emotionally react to things we can't see.
- It never feels like they are telling the whole truth.

So, why oh why in the proverbial audition room, would it behoove any of us to dress ourselves up with a perfect line reading and the right song? It's so easy to go down the route of being the good girl or boy. We show up and do the right thing. We sign with the right agency, we get published in the most traditional way, we study our instrument with the best mentor money can buy. But the problem is there is no right way to do any of this, there is only an authentic way to do this. This makes most perfectionists (myself included) squirmy. It also makes us liars. Most of us want to head for the hills when we can't do things the right way. But to be able to shift energies and move creative mountains, you have to break your perfectionism habit just like you would put down any other drug. And there is only way to break your perfectionism habit: really, badly, irrevocably mess up. Hey, and while you're at it, allow people to dislike you. How's that one feel?

You've got to fall. On your face. Hard. It needs to hurt. You need to lose. You need to be cut. You need to be rejected. You need to be kept out of the party. And then? You notice you're still breathing, thinking, doing, but with lower expectations of approval. And lower expectations of approval means your free will has come out of hiding. Understand what I'm suggesting: lower expectations of others' approval means higher expectations of your own. You take the value off of them and put it onto you. Unless you are zenned-out from the first day of your life, I believe this is a continuing lesson that will show up again and again.

Ask yourself, when have I faced rock bottom? When did I think shit really hit the fan? Remember those times and then ask yourself what you did *next.* There is your light. There is your instinct. You unshackled yourself from measuring *up* so you could fill *in.* You said, *to hell with all of that because I actually believe this.* Are you scared of letting go that much? If you are, I am right there with you. But from the other side, this much I know: You cannot step foot into the party and believe any real impact can be had from your work if you don't know who you are.

Finally Arriving

If you have traded in your fearlessness for confident vulnerability and checked your perfectionism at the door, congratulations. You now have a standing chance at changing the energy in the room. You have battled your way against obstacles, some manufactured and some true, and given yourself permission to arrive at the party.

These are the moments when I believe the artist is a hero. Those moments might not amount to a role or a paycheck, but they settle deep in your marrow, manifested as the glory of doing your work. Of standing in your moment without apology or overzealous assuredness. Of knowing that despite the ridiculous crapshoot of a business, you showed up to be seen.

Being seen holds an inordinate amount of power.

Being seen means standing in your own skin, with your own insecurities, frailties, faults, and saying, *I'm here and I'm enough. Now let's make something worthwhile.*

Inner Validation

When I started researching material for this book, I asked people what they found the most challenging about being a creative. The answers were varied and funny and nuanced for sure, but about 70 percent of the responses that came back cited lack of inner validation. Everyone seemed to be asking the question, *How do I know when I am good enough?*

So like a good and organized writer, as I began this book, I listed all the topics I wanted to write about, the ones I had already written, and the feedback from my investigating. I had lists upon lists of ideas, but when it came time to write about inner validation, I became all sorts of blocked.

What insight could I possibly offer when I struggle with this so much myself? And then of course, my next thought was, *you're resisting. It's time to write.*

Everyone wants to be validated. Everyone wants to be affirmed. And if you've lived any amount of time at all in this uncertain world then you know that outside validation never compares to that deep knowing in your gut that you are absolutely capable. We want the good reviews and we want to land the jobs, but beneath the layers of shiny accomplishment, if our still small voice doesn't say *you done good, kid* then nothing else really matters. So how do we get there? How do we get to the point where we know what we're doing is good, valuable, or even just enough?

It's not simple and it's simple: get to your flow. Your flow state is your truth, your unconscious being that radiates without self-judgment or critique. It's the silencer of noisy self-sabotaging opinion and the opener of essence. It's the state you exist in when you're ready to take off, with the right blend of fear and confidence. It's the brave voyage inward. It's the moment we release our heavily-cloaked should-be selves and trade her in for some really real realness.

Being in your flow is not just a mushy creative expression, this is a scientifically backed phenomenon that explains how creatives from jazz musicians to extreme athletes accomplish incredible feats of skill, agility and magic. Your brain is literally transforming, learning and enhancing itself within the flow state. So let's go there.

The F Word

Flow can be a blend of different ingredients for everyone, but at the bottom it's all about losing yourself. It is letting go of the conscious self because all of your energy is poured into the task at hand. This is decidedly different from the mindless-numbed-out-unconsciousness we experience from time to time. It's not the morning subway commute when all of a sudden we've made our transfer and don't know how we ended up there. It's not mindlessly brushing your teeth and then being unable to remember whether you did it or not. That is not flow. That is losing yourself in the back of your head, not within the moment. There is a stark difference between being stuck in your head and being opened up in your being. When you get to the end of an eight-hour day of work and think, we're done already? Wait I got more in me! *That's* flow. The difference?

Unconscious numbness neglects to challenge us.
Flow challenges us to push out of our comfort zone toward our most creative selves.

The First Ten Years

Once we understand the difference between checking out and checking in, it gets much easier to figure out how to do the latter. If flow exists when we are doing something an inch or two past our comfort level, all we need to do is keep putting challenges in front of our determined little noses. The more we are complacent, the more we are unconscious. The more we are stimulated, the more we flow.

Be honest with yourself. Do you do the same thing day in and day out and expect to feel a sense of flow from tracing and retracing the same old steps? I'm not suggesting we all fly off to Europe and go backpacking for 90 days (although, more power to ya...). It can be simpler than that. I used to sit at my computer every day to troll Facebook, try to think of something clever for Twitter, read an article or two. When I decided to write a book, I had never committed to something so challenging. Now as I sat down to my computer, I wasn't just opening it up to go numb, I was opening it up to expand. For me, writing a book was a new (read: brain-happy-making) experience, so I had to push past my easy edges and rise up to the new challenge. All of a sudden, the space disappeared, hunger disappeared, anxiety disappeared. Maybe I was opening my computer like I had done a million times before, but because writing was so much more challenging than trolling, the minute my fingers started typing, I dropped in and opened up.

Were my first words masterpiece-level? Not a chance in hell. But they were down. Challenge accepted. I had gotten a small taste of flow and I wanted more. I wanted to pour everything out on the page and then deal with it later. Detaching felt damn good. So while it might be scary to try something in a slightly different way, that's just your unconscious mind making up stories again. What's real, what's absolutely true, what's been proven through history and neuroscience, is that when you do something slightly difficult but matched appropriately with your skill level, to the point where all your abilities have to come to attention to creatively solve or conquer your beast, you feel good. Your brain releases dopamine.

You want to get high? Get to work. Have you ever felt runner's high? A moment where your body feels suspended and easy even as it performs a difficult task? That's flow. Ever get into a really clever, funny, popping conversation where you're not considering what to say next but you're just allowing a natural riff to take you forward? That's flow. Ever get new direction in an audition room or have to cold read a side (performing material you've never seen before) and feel more connected to that material than your over-rehearsed monologue? That's flow. Ever pitch your idea to investors and find the right words come out and land on the room with unstoppable effectiveness? That's flow.

Flow Can't Be Chased

The silly part about flow is that the more we try to access it, the more it eludes us. It's not unattainable, it's just that *trying* has to do with accomplishing. Flow has to do with being. Flow is balance. If you tip too far over onto the effortful, desperate-to-succeed side, you become blocked. Everything you do is under a microscope. You have no ability to play. Your spontaneity gets squashed under the heavy foot of judgment. No fun. If on the other hand, you tip too far over to a completely relaxed state, with nothing at stake (our subway commute for example), you come up with nothing exciting, novel or fresh. Maintaining this balance means you are equal parts passionate and relaxed, stoked and calm, lit up and dropped in.

That balance between trying too hard and not trying at all is crucial, but it doesn't have to be tricky.

Have you seen clips of Larry Bird playing basketball? This man is a textbook example of flow state. When he is on that court, he is unquestionably connected to the ball. He dribbles the ball with startling ease, taps the ball, punches the ball, flips it behind him, scoops it off the floor at the last second. He knows where every opponent and every teammate is and where they *will* be. His connection leads him to be open because he's not pummeling through his opponents, he's flowing with them. His energy rebounds from one side of the court to the next. This guy is so good he rebounds on his own shot, all the while making it look effortless. He is not chasing flow, he is flowing. He is not chasing the ball, he is the ball.

To find your flow...

Go for a walk or work out. The research linking walking (even just pacing) and creativity is astonishing.

Meditate. The fMRI scans of brains in meditation and flow are surprisingly similar. Use this meditative state to remind your brain of how it can easily drop into being without judging.

Do something new. Maybe it has nothing to do with your current project, but trying to master something new will stimulate your synapses and remind you how good it feels to creatively solve a problem.

Get yourself a change of scene. This could be taking a vacation or moving from your desk to a new part of the house. Trade in your stale setting for something novel and new, and your brain will thank you.

Learn something. Part of creativity is simply taking bits and pieces of information and connecting them to render something completely new. Sometimes, you just need to fill the well and get some new information in your gray matter. From there, connections are bound to flow.

Why Your Flow Is Your Validation

Flow is imperative to doing your work. Flow is imperative to validating yourself because it is the only time you can objectively step back without overcompensating or underrating. Your flow state is access. It's access to a bigger power, a bigger picture, the best part of yourself, unveiled and untouchable by anyone but you. That, my dear artistic compatriots, is power. No one else can access your flow. No one else has the key. If you don't go in and unlock it, it remains hidden from the world forever. Turn the key, step in, and unleash yourself. Let the words or paint or choices pass through you but not because of you. Rather, because you allowed yourself to get out of the way for a moment. You don't have to become creative, you are creative. Get your mind out of the way and just, flow.

Get It Down: Your Energy is Your Currency

What energy do you seek out?

_____

_____

_____

What energy do you think you have?

_____

_____

_____

When do you take on energy that doesn't reflect you? Who are you with? What are you doing?

_____

_____

_____

What is the experience you want your audience to have when they engage with your work?

_____

_____

_____

When do you find yourself going numb and unconscious? How can you make that experience fresh?

_____

_____

_____

When have you found yourself in flow state? What was the sensory experience around you? How can you recreate that regularly?

_____

_____

_____

Your distractions,
unconscious or not,
are choices.

SIX:
DISTRACTIONS (BOTH KINDS)

There are two kinds of distractions: one keeps you from your daily work (small) and one keeps you from your life (big).

The Small Kind

If like me, you use tabs in your Internet browser, then you know the small kind.

Small distractions creep up on everyone. Knowing exactly what I want to get done and then going off and doing something completely different is fifty percent of how I get my work on the page. I open every social media account I have. I check how many likes I got on Instagram. I look at my upcoming schedule for the week. Each of these unconscious moves takes me further and further away from what I sat down to do: write.

Everyone has a different take on why this happens. Why can't we just sit down and do what we say we're going to do? All signs in the universe point to one of two answers:

You really don't want to do the thing.
You really want to do the thing.

How do you know which reason is keeping you from your work? The trouble is you won't know until you actually do the thing. Until you dive face first into the work, you have no idea what you want to do. I have written tens of thousands of words only to find out it was the wrong thing to write. But it wasn't a waste. Knowing what you don't want to do is just as valuable as knowing what you want to do. It's all information, and better information about yourself will make you better.

The small distraction messiness exposes itself in a variety of ways.

- When you find yourself distracted, and somewhere in your gut, you know you really want to pursue the book or painting or song or new business, <u>you unconsciously go searching for reasons not to pursue it</u>. You scan your to-do lists and your schedule to find one specific and immovable reason why you just can't sit down and get to work. Your distraction is planned, effortful and rational. It boldly guides you away from the commitment. It shoos you into tedious chores that you need to check off before you actually tackle the art you planned on making today. Email is a great indicator of how much you want to pursue something. The more you check your email in the middle of "working," chances are the more you want to get to work.

- On the other hand, sometimes you know in your gut you want to do this thing more than anything else in the world, so <u>your mind suddenly freaks out and goes unconscious</u>. You get glazed over. This hazy unconsciousness is a big old red flag. You sit down to write, and all of a sudden you're online shopping; you want to have a significant conversation with your partner, and all of a sudden your mind starts writing your grocery list; you want to go to an audition with a new monologue, but instead you go look in the fridge for a snack. Do any of these sound familiar? Cloudiness is resistance.

- The last form unconsciousness takes is <u>over-productivit</u>y. It delights in making you believe you are so productive, you can't stop, you won't stop, you are racing a million miles a minute and before you know it you've started eight projects and finished none. We never go to the frontier of ourselves. We get far enough down the road and instead of doubling down in our work, we make a turn. Just to look, because maybe this way is better. We don't stake out territory in our creativity, we merely vacation there. We close in the possibilities around us, thick like a winter blanket, shielding us from the wind chill of exposure and the opportunity to know ourselves better. Because what if we're disappointing? What if we don't like who we are? What if we don't get followers?

Unconscious distractions are our fears' way of manhandling our spirit. We never do practice our ukulele because we're constantly forgetting. Even when it's sitting right in front of us for most of the day.

The Big Kind

The big kind of distraction is a master of disguise. It makes itself seem productive, it convinces you that it will help your bigger goals, it shrouds itself with fake prestige. Steven Pressfield says these distractions can turn into "shadow careers" and he's right. They hide in plain sight. We all want absolutes. We all want security and assuredness. Our creative work feels fragile and incoherent so we look under every rock for something solid. The thing about life is, no matter who you are or what you do, there is no such thing as security. Stability is a sham. It doesn't actually exist. So when we go searching *out there* to find something that resembles security, we run away from all the things that actually have the power to make us feel grounded *right here.*

Case in point: My shadow career was that direct sales job selling cosmetics I took when I was 27. I spent almost $2000 to stock up on products I could sell at parties. The day my first shipment came in, I was sitting in my 400-square-foot apartment, surrounded by pink little boxes, excited and nervous and ignoring a nagging feeling in the back of my head that maybe I should be working on my audition material instead of organizing eye shadows. But everything was packaged so beautifully, I had a plan in place, and let's be honest, I needed a win. I believed this sales job would catapult me to success. I thought it would give me financial abundance, it would use my talents in a way that pursuing an acting career did not always do, and because of its flexibility, it would allow me to make every audition my little heart desired. Bottom line, I believed this job would assure that I could act *forever.* And guess what I did much less of so I could pursue the success of that sales job? Audition.

There were elements I liked: helping other people, inspiring other people, feeling free to do my work on my own, not being in an office, making my own hours. But there were more elements that I disliked: working on commission, getting paid off of other people's work, always having to hustle, being on the phone all the time, feeling embarrassed because I represented a brand that wasn't me.

Feeling embarrassed should have been my biggest indicator. That was a tough pill to swallow. I was in sales, I had to put myself out there, but I felt embarrassed every time I did. Why didn't I take that sign? My job had become an unconscious distraction. It wasn't the benefits of the job that I was compelled by, it was the fact that it stole all of the energy I could have given to acting and put it on something else. I unconsciously threw myself into a different career trajectory because my fear manhandled my spirit. My resistance was so strong that I tricked myself into believing that planning for a career was the same as making one happen. I allowed people to convince me that this sales job would support me in the future when all it did was keep me from what I really wanted to do now. Hell, I convinced myself that this was the only way I would ever make it as an actress - by not being an actress.

A lot of writing, therapy and soul-searching led me to ask these questions:

When did I decide that being okay and being a creative were mutually exclusive?

When did I decide that I couldn't make money through being a creative?

When did I decide that it would always be a struggle?

The key here: decide. Our distractions are decisions, unconscious though they may be. They cover up something deeply manifested in our gut: a fear, a doubt, something we've heard others say. Those unconscious triggers are not the truth. Yes, they feel real as hell, but they are imaginative theories based on the fakest of the fake. Distractions are lies.

Looking back on my experience in sales, I knew I didn't feel like myself, but I didn't yet have the emotional backbone to take matters into my own hands. Craig was the one who finally said, enough. And though I initially fought him, when I too accepted that I needed to quit, I came to feel a flood of relief. It was over. I wasn't going to save my acting career by being a salesperson. It was distracting me from actually having a career. As painful as it was, to step out of that darkness and into the light was truly one of the best moments of my life.

A Final Note on Distractions

I think it is decidedly important to say that distractions of both kinds are dangerous. No, not irritating, not annoying; they carry pure, unadulterated danger because when you go too far down the distraction highway, you end up in a sketchy part of town. You start saying things that don't sound like you, because you aren't considering your words, you aren't responding with your thoughts, you aren't being deliberate in your actions. Because you're not deciding for yourself, you're letting the rest of the world stamp you with what they'd like to get out of you. To do anything significant, you need a vision. You cannot have a vision if you're not awake.

Remember:

Distractions are the mind's way of staying safe, plain and average.
Distractions keep you small, blinders on, ignorant to life on the outside.
Life on the outside is where you're going to get some crazy good inspiration. Don't miss it.
Distractions make you fat, sometimes.
Distractions make you sad, sometimes.
Distractions kill creativity.
Distractions keep you bored.
Distractions keep you isolated.
Distractions are not play or rest, they are soul-suckers.

Get It Down: Wandering Back Home

What does your instinct feel like?

_____

_____

_____

When have you known something was wrong or right?

_____

_____

_____

Where do you spend your time the most during the day?

_____

_____

_____

What habits contribute to your feeling of contentment? What habits discourage you?

_____

_____

_____

What are your habits keeping you from?

_____

_____

_____

**Why don't you want to do that now? How can you do
that instead?**

_____

_____

_____

KNOWING YOUR WORK

Follow your
sadness
to discover your
joy.

SEVEN: Following Your Sadness

I am a big believer that what you sling out into the world directly corresponds with what you should expect to receive from it. There was a period of my life I like to title *Desperate For The Answers And Why Aren't Things Going My Way And Was It Supposed To Be This Hard And AHHHHHHHH?*, (alternate title: *My 20s*), when I would hurl a lot of anxiety and defensiveness into the world and it would boomerang back to me in the form of rejection. Lots of rejection. I was good enough to get to final callbacks, but I just couldn't land the gig. Instead of looking inward, for a long time I blamed. And then I got bitter. And then I got a teensy tiny bit hostile.

My actions and behavior during this period showed the world three things, two true and one false:

a)   I did not have my shit together (true)
b)   I did not have anything of value to add (false)
c)   my ego was at once so delicate that even the smallest rejection felt unfathomably harsh and so massive that it overshadowed the joy I derived from being creative (sadly, true)

I have accomplished many great things of which I am immensely proud, but I have also had many disappointments, almosts, close-but-no-cigar-moments, and these setbacks used to drain any enthusiasm left in my tank. I made it to plenty of final callbacks only to be met with radio silence from the auditors who had seemed so enthused by my shuffle ball changes in the sweaty audition room just days before. I did not land a real acting job for three years.

I sat in my little apartment in Brooklyn while Craig was performing at the Alabama Shakespeare Festival for the good part of a year, and prayed to God, tears streaming down my face, to give me a different

117

passion in life. Not one of my finer moments, but I want you to understand something: If things aren't going so well and you're sad right now, I see you.

When I was swimming around in my self-pity I blamed it on the business. Naming the business as my biggest problem meant I could situate myself as the victim of it. Blaming the business allowed me to disengage from what was really hurting, and what I knew to be true underneath my sullen whining: I was getting in my own way.

It's Only a Day Away

Around 2011, *Annie* was being revived on Broadway, and I had to be in it. I wasn't trying to fulfill any childhood dreams of singing "Tomorrow;" if I was aspiring to be any famous redhead I was gunning for Ariel not Annie. I had to be in *Annie* because I had been desperate to work with the production's choreographer. I had been following his work for years, I took his master classes, and auditioned for him every time he had a new show coming up. His material was fresh; it was unexpected and it embraced storytelling in a way that most choreographers neglected. The way he used movement on stage inspired me to tell stories in the same way, and so when the chance to work with him arose, I had to go in. Without an agent, on my own accord, I showed up for the cattle call. Hundreds of girls came to dance for a few spots in the ensemble. I got through rounds of callbacks and was finally dancing for my choreographic hero. Every cut was an inch closer to getting into this show. I saw my life turning around, the answer being sent down from heaven above. I thought for sure I was about to make my Broadway debut.

We were in the dance portion of the callback, sweat-drenched from learning a technically difficult rendition of "I Think I'm Gonna Like It Here." He sat at the front of the room, in all black, hunched in deep thought over our resumes. All the girls had finished dancing and we were standing on the side. My red leotard was soaked to crimson. After a few moments he looked up at the group and he asked two other girls and me to dance for a second time. This can mean a lot of different things at dance calls. It might mean you stood in the back, they didn't get to see you and wanted to give you a fair shot; it could mean they weren't sure if they liked you or not and needed to see you do it again; it could mean they wanted to give you a note and see if you could take it because they were very interested in you. I knew I had to pull out all the stops. I knew I had to land every turn, create a story arc in thirty seconds of choreography, and seem super fun to work with without seeming desperate. This was my opportunity. I gave myself a quick pep talk, took center stage and nailed it. I landed the turns, told the story, appeared to be a delight. In my humble opinion, I was dripping Broadway credentials. I watched him review my resume a few times, looking back and forth between it and me. I couldn't wait to call my mom and tell her the good news. They thanked everyone for coming and said they were about to make a cut. They read the names of the girls they were keeping; out of the 15 girls there, only three were sent home.

I was one of them.

I managed to squeak out my requisite "thank you" as I grabbed my dance bag and took my walk of shame. As the door closed behind me, I heard everyone else in the room begin to learn another sequence. The shuffling of bodies and some muffled laughter were acute reminders that I was most definitely not invited to that party. Trying to hold back tears until I could get out onto 8th Avenue, I sprinted out of the building. Just to add insult to injury, I was headed to my bartending gig.

The First Ten Years

On the way there, I stopped in the café I reserved for special occasions: nailed auditions and failed auditions. It had cupcakes the size of my face and if I didn't have to fit into a costume, might as well drown myself in carrot cake. I called my mom, not to revel in victory but to announce defeat. "I'm quitting show business," I told her as I licked cream cheese frosting off my finger. "If I was any good I would have booked a Broadway show by now," I said through sloppy tear-filled bites. "No, it's done. I'm never going through this bullshit again."

What can I say? I have a flair for the dramatic.

Instead of acknowledging that my sadness was real, but that it would pass, I acted as if Sadness and Disappointment would be my default modes for the rest of my life. What I didn't realize right away is that our sadness is directionally intuitive. When I calmed down and started uncovering why I was miserable over not booking a show I had no real attachment to anyway, I realized I was grieving the lost opportunity to create. All I really wanted to do was create. I wanted to act. I wanted to work. I wanted to be on stage. In other words, my sadness pointed toward my joy.

We have to let go of the mistaken belief that if you love what you're pursuing, every part of it will feel wonderful and warm and fuzzy. Once we can do that, we can spend some time with our sadness. And instead of settling there and blaming that awful feeling on the outside world, by poking around to uncover what's really at the root, we find our passion. Our calling. Our joy. Then things start to move. Things start to shift.

It took me a few more years to figure this out, but I felt sad because I wanted to be a part of something big. I felt sad because I wanted a challenge. I felt sad because being on stage makes me feel alive and present. So when I objectively dug into the sadness, I could articulate what made me feel joyful:

Having a community.
Pushing out of my comfort zone.
Feeling alive and present.

Years later, I discovered that dancing in the ensemble of a Broadway show is not a prerequisite for those things. Following my sadness helped bring me closer to my real identity; it made all the cuts and rejections seem arbitrary. My joy was much deeper and wider than dancing in the ensemble. I wanted more.

I didn't know exactly what yet, and let me tell you, it's really scary to start shifting your dreams. But to be a successful creative, you have to be honest with your ever-evolving self. You can't operate from anyone else's set of values or definition of joy. And you can't fix your happiness on ephemeral things. Had I booked *Annie,* it would have eventually closed. I would have been out of work again. But the feeling of being present and alive and pushed out of my comfort zone - that I could craft on my own.

It's hard for me to believe that any creative could happily exist checking accomplishment after accomplishment off the list without satisfying some of that soul-feeding joy that comes from deeply knowing who you are. We all know people who are incredibly successful yet profoundly bitter. Wildly ambitious yet deeply discouraged. Financially stable yet fragile as hell. If we don't pay attention to our sadness, we can't cultivate our joy. And the resilience and buoyancy of joy is the key to staying afloat in any creative pursuit.

Get It Down: Find the Joy

In your life, when have you felt real sadness?

_____

_____

_____

Why did you feel sad? Be specific here. If it's because you didn't get a job - what was it about that job that you wanted? Security? To feel valued? Power? Prestige? There is no wrong answer, be as honest as possible. Stay with this one for a while until something clicks and feels spot on.

_____

_____

_____

_____

_____

_____

How would that particular instance have made you joyful?

_____

_____

_____

_____

_____

_____

When have you experienced joy in your life?

_____

_____

_____

_____

_____

_____

How can you create that joy in your life today? For example, if your joy is connected to feeling valued, maybe you take a long luxurious walk to value your down time, or you paint your nails, or call a friend who needs you. Be creative and courageous when coming up with ways to feel joy. Don't shut anything down. Be open to the fact that joy comes in many forms, and often, not in ways we expect.

_____

_____

_____

Your daydreams are guideposts to creating the life you want.

EIGHT : CREATING THE LIFESTYLE, AKA, LIVIN' THE LIFE

In my childhood dreams of being an actress, I always pictured myself drinking coffee and wearing a scarf in downtown Manhattan. What that image has to do with acting eludes me, but the amazing part is that it's not too far off from the image of my real daily life. Lots of coffee. Lots of scarves. Usually downtown. Your dream probably didn't look quite the same, but you did have some other whimsical image in your head. Future you, living the dream, artistically satisfied and extremely well-dressed. Actors dream of mornings in minimalist Brooklyn lofts where diffused light floats in across the neighborhood rooftops to make everything feel a little more hopeful. We dream of afternoon café meet-ups to review scripts with up-and-coming writers and directors whose enthusiasm gives us goosebumps, and we dream of nights recreating the La Vie Bohéme scene from *RENT,* because what if money lost its value and we replaced it with exuberance and community and the belief that making art is going to be what saves all of us?

Maybe that last part is just me.

But my point is we each have a vision that romanticizes what it actually means to be a creative. It's easy to discount these visions as pipe dreams, but when we hash them out, we can see that they are actually guideposts. They tell us how making our art a reality might make us feel. In the process of building a career, we will constantly evolve and so will the image of our artist persona. Those initial images are anchored to something deep and authentic in us. They're attached to some desire that we probably couldn't exorcise if we tried. So we have to do our best to try and recreate those images in our real lives.

First thing's first: we need to decode our vision. What was it about my downtown coffee-drinking drama queen that appealed to my younger, visionary self? When I see the woman I dreamt of being, I see someone who is grounded but free. I see an artist unafraid of uncertainty and owning it; she goes her own way, she chooses to be an original whether she's commercially successful or not, and she takes responsibility for everything that shows up in her life. I see a community of artists that inspire and push her to make meaningful work. I see comrades. I see collaboration. I see unexpected opportunities in her every day. I see magic.

Let's start there.

Creating the Magic

I used to audition with one song. I liked how I sounded singing it. It showed my range and personality. Any musical theatre acting teacher in New York will tell you what's important: range and personality. I thought that because I liked it, I would perform it well. And I did, for a little bit, and then I started sounding stale. I wasn't paying attention to the words I was saying. I sang from muscle memory. It was safe.

I used to write for too many blogs. Paid and unpaid, out my words went. I was scrounging the bottom of the imaginative reservoir for inspiration and came up only with hyperbole and cliché. I couldn't catch my vision because I was moving too fast, exhausting my creative energy for very little payoff, and with not-great results.

I used to operate by this silly principle that *if it worked once, it will work again!* When I realized my auditions and my writing were all drying up and I was losing whatever magical effect my work had before, I developed a practical plan to get the magic back:

Stop.

Come On, Do It, Be A Quitter

For the first time ever, I took time away from auditioning. For ten years I had gone to almost every call that seemed appropriate for me. If the breakdown for the audition asked for one skill I had, I showed up. If they asked for a 5'9" forty-five-year-old African American ukulele player, I'd think, UKULELE! BINGO! My brain didn't always work. When this was going on, I never turned down my agents, even if what they sent me in for wasn't actually turning me on. Those were the years when I thought not getting a job meant I wasn't working hard enough. If only I could just sing better. Kick my legs higher. Lose more weight. Go to more auditions. Make more connections. Have more energy. Be a bright shining star of musical theatre potential. I could do it. I could do it. I could do it. I was having my proverbial Jesse Spano freak out moment. For a little longer than necessary.

So, for six solid months I just stopped. I stopped checking the breakdowns, stopped asking my friends if they were planning on going to this audition or that one, stopped caring when people posted about their glorious theatrical success on Facebook, stopped believing that Broadway was the answer and anything short of that was failure. I stopped all of those bad emotional habits because I stepped away. I backed down. I said, *fine you win*. I went on vacation. I didn't care.

The act of not caring is revolutionary and it is vital to good work. There have been moments in my career when I have said that I didn't care and then stormed out of the audition center with resentment building up in my veins. I have rationalized why booking that job would have been more of a headache than a triumph and then silently grieved for the performance I could have given. Saying you don't care is not the same as not caring, and it's important to distinguish between the two.

I could not get to a place of giving zero shits unless I completely stepped back. I had to put up my walls. I went so far as telling Craig and my best friends and my parents that I was leaving the business. I was resolute. It wasn't like all those other times before. This was for realsies.

The best thing about not caring is that you can absorb a lot more information. You see a beautiful piece of clothing and notice the colors and patterns and stitching detail instead of analyzing how it would work in an audition. You hear a great new piece of music and stop scheming ways to get your best friend to transpose it into an audition cut. You meet new people and stop viewing them as potential business contacts. You start going to parties for fun and stop reasoning that the only point in going is to network. Not caring means better living. Better living means the magic can happen.

Better living is what got us into whatever we're into in the first place. It was as easy as being captivated. We allowed ourselves to be swept up by something outside of us. We just loved what we loved. We didn't scheme. We listened. Simple. No exertion. We just let the information in and allowed the creative time bomb to go off when it was good and ready.

When we start feeling the giant balloon of our magic deflate and all we're left with is the used up, rubbery shell, we have to step away. We have to stop trying to trap that magic inside our shriveled balloon. We can't will the air into it, we need tools. Only once we've stepped away to go get the hose can we fill it back up.

Magic happens...

When we feel open: This goes hand in hand with vulnerability, but it's another step. It's allowing yourself to be influenced, to be written upon, to be changed by things outside of your control.

When we trust in our ability to do our work: We have to know that when we sit down to do our work, the right words, decisions and energy will come. Once we're open, we need to just forge ahead, and worry about revising and editing and perfecting later.

When we simply sit down to work: We just have to cop a squat. Or get on our feet. Or get in the audition line. Or call the investor. Or do the necessary thing to put us in the space of our work. It seems simple, but this might be the hardest thing to do.

When we feel safe enough to take a risk: We need to scare ourselves with enough out-of-the-comfort-zone work to feel like we're pushing forward. We need to feel like the world could shift under our feet, and we need to use that extra adrenaline to make newer, bolder choices. We need to figure it out as we go.

When we rest: Getting yourself to the workspace is hard, but getting yourself out in the open air of play can be harder. Just like your physical muscles, your magic muscle can't grow if you don't give it time to heal, repair, fill back up.

Creating the Threshold

In the trancelike dream state of early adulthood, most of the time it's the *having of things* that fill our fantasies of our futures selves. We have a loft, we have a bookshelf overflowing with books, we have a steady paycheck that assures we can afford both of those things. We see the environment. But how much is our current space a conscious reflection of what we want? Some people nail this, but if you're like me, you've gotten hand-me-down after hand-me-down and you're into saving a buck so you reason that *well, this desk isn't my jam, but it's free so it stays.*

I'm not saying you need to hop over to West Elm and redecorate (although, take me with you if you do), but I am saying that the environment you create for yourself as an artist needs to be conscious and intentional.

If all of those visuals from my fantasy made me covet the feeling of being both grounded and free, then those feelings should make their way into my work. And if they should be in my work, then it will serve me to create a space in order to elicit the feelings of being both grounded and free.

The best way to get this environment without paying an interior decorator is to create a threshold. An in and an out. You don't have to do this with furniture, you could do this with time. I write my best pieces in the early morning hours. It's something about the light that comes into our kitchen. It's backyard city light; it's diluted and cool and oddly still. It lulls me into my writing zone. I'll wake up early, close the kitchen doors, put on the French press - I've created my threshold. I set boundaries to protect my space. At around 11 a.m., the environment evaporates, because I run out of steam or have other obligations or the light gets too bright and I find it difficult to concentrate, but I know I can step over that threshold every morning and be in a fantasy-like work-producing environment.

Whether you get your work done in a little corner nook of your apartment, at the local coffee shop, on a park bench, at your parents' house, in a cold, dark basement - one thing remains the same: the space needs to speak to you. The space you create for your work is all about the threshold. Once you define where the threshold is (a door being shut, a candle being lit, a Spotify playlist being turned on, the Facebook being turned off), you step over it and can begin your work. When you cross that threshold into your creative domain, you must rally all the energy you can get to keep you there for as long as it takes. The more you create the environment, the more you learn about your process. And the more you learn about your process, the more agility you'll have to approach your material.

Creating the Influence

Influence. For many artists, this is the apex of our fantasy. We dream of our work being so influential that we can effect change and create our own opportunities. In an artist's mind, influence is more red-hot than money. We know we can make money when we have to because we are resourceful, but creating influence depends on the right message landing on the right people at the right time. That can feel unmanageable and chaotic, so self-doubt and angst burrow right in under our skin. But influence doesn't have to be so hard to attain. All we need to do? Be influenced.

What I Learned From An Eyebrow

Most likely due to a good deed in a past life, one summer the theatre gods allowed me to act alongside Liz Larsen, and she changed my perspective on influence. This Tony-nominated musical theatre superhero allowed herself to be influenced. Maybe this doesn't sound astonishing, but looking at the length and prestige of her career, understanding the kinds of stars she was used to working with, seeing her work with both ease and exactness, you could understand if she had wanted to close herself off from anything less than magical. But the brilliance of her work, the way she became such an influencing and charismatic player in New York City was because she kept her currents open. If anything was going to land, it was going to land on her.

I learned this when we were performing in a scene in which we had to freeze while staring each other down as an extended joke happened around us. The whole thing was absurd. We were in the middle of a hilarious scene and anyone who has been to an organized religious service knows that when something is funny and you're not supposed to laugh, it gets funnier. Not laughing was unimaginable but that was our task. During a particularly electrified performance one night, the audience was alert and sensing every shift we made on stage. After one of the big bits, when the whole audience swelled with laughter and then quieted down to hear what ridiculous antic was coming next, one audience member let out a guffaw. It was so loud and so joyous, the whole audience erupted again. And we just held. And stayed straight face. Our abs quivered with the tension from not joining in the release.

After the show, when we were chatting about the moment, superhero said, "The only thing I could do was just keep repeating *I love you, I love you, I love you*. I just thought, *I love her so much*." That's what she did to stay in the moment. She leaned into it. She pressed deeper into what was happening by connecting even more deeply to me, her counterpart. She kept herself from laughing by staying with a thought that connected her to the stage and to me.

Then I revealed my tactic. I had been avoiding laughter by fixating on the left corner of her eyebrow.

That right there is the difference between an influential being and a less influential being: openness.

I moved no mountains by saying I looked at her eyebrow to avoid the moment. She completely transformed me by admitting she dug her heels in. This woman is all kinds of talented, but I imagine this availability to the moment helped make her an influential force in the theatre community.

There is a tacit adjustment we make when we open up. We stop letting fear rule our actions. Being open assumes that life will come in and land. It assumes the uncertainty of it all will fill up the empty spaces between our control and our plans and we're okay with that. Those two moves we make, to open up and then to relax away from fear, are what make our stories effect change and give birth to influence.

To be influenced means you are open. You are unabashedly present. No walls are up, all the light is let in. Those are the exact conditions necessary to become influential yourself. Influence has less to do with gripping power, and more to do with subtle presence.

You are influential because...
> You see others' truth.
> You communicate authenticity.
> You go beyond what's flatly in front of you to
> > create something new, out of nothing.
> You trust yourself.
> You trust others.
> You choose to see more in the world than the

Average Joe.

Sidenote: If you're starting to get a little fidgety at the talk of influence, stay with me for a moment. Every human being is already influential. That influence could be bad or good, but we are each influential, and have the potential to be *stunningly* influential. You *have to* step into this to change the world. You *have to* believe you have something of value to say so that we can benefit from your experience of the world. No one else will go through life seeing how you see, hearing how you hear, loving how you love. If you think influence isn't something you should strive to have, you're missing the point of uniqueness, and we miss out big time. Don't hoard all your goodness to yourself. Let it out.

Get It Down: Fantasy and Reality

In your fantasy life, what environment would you work in? What would it feel like?

_____

_____

_____

What are the thresholds that you already use on a daily basis, if any? Do they work?

_____

_____

_____

How can you incorporate the feeling of your fantasy environment into your reality?

_____

_____

_____

Who influences you in your field the most? What do you love about their work? What gets you fired up about how they do what they do?

_____

_____

_____

What is the most surprising way someone has influenced you? How do you want to influence others around you?

_____

_____

_____

_____

_____

_____

When you find yourself in creative chaos, your intuition is your anchor.

NINE:
DEVELOPING
INTUITION

In my first acting class in college, I had a ton of questions about the first scene I was assigned. Was my character upset or was she playing a game? Was she as manipulative as I thought? How should I say this one line? And how about the next? And the next? I stayed after class to ask my professor these questions and expected her to give me the right answers, and then show me how to find the right answer every single time.

Now, every creative knows there are no right or wrong choices; there are only effective or less effective choices. In any case, binaries are unhelpful and there are no answers. It's the nauseating and fun part of being a creative: who knows?! But in my 18-year-old brain, I assumed that there was one way to do it and (because I loved following the rules) all I needed to do was learn what that was and execute. It existed outside of me and I just had to discover it and play by the rules. I was good at that.

I could blame my naiveté on being a teenager, but the truth is that even now, when I know that I'm the only one who holds the answers to my questions (see Chapter One), there are still times when my intuition dissolves and I hunt for the right answer. It must be somewhere out there. Outside of myself.

Following My Gut Out The Door

During my stint with the cosmetics brand, my emotional stakes were getting higher and the responsibilities were growing. I was rising in the ranks and more was being demanded of me. Around that same time, I booked my first acting gig after a three-year drought. I had acknowledged my sadness and my joy so I could let myself enjoy the audition process again. Now the world was opening up.

The First Ten Years

When we open up, new possibilities open up. We can't follow every path, so we have to measure our opportunities against our dreams to know what we should hold onto and what we should let go. I considered what was in front of me with the sales job. The whole appeal of working in direct sales was that I could still make extra money even if I booked a job that took me to different parts of the country. If the gig didn't quite pay the bills, the sale of a couple facial cleansers could. I had booked an acting contract with a decent paycheck, but like all shows, it was temporary. I thought, maybe it was smart to hold onto the makeup gig as a back-up. So I packed my dance shoes and my product and hopped on a train.

I got to the gig, excited out of my mind to hit the stage for a solid four months of work performing four different productions in a row after years of auditioning without getting a bite. I was playing parts, I was singing, I was dancing. That summer expanded me to the capacity I knew I had all along. It was thrilling and I was so grateful (like happy tears, joy filling up my heart every day, pinch-me-this-is-my-life kind of grateful). The cosmetics stayed hidden at the back of my closet in the cast housing where I lived. My box of money-making makeup wasn't even opened. I didn't want to look at it. Pairing lipstick to lip gloss just didn't feel as exciting to me now that I was doing what I actually loved to do.

One day during rehearsals, we were going over the opening number. We had been dancing for four days straight and my body wasn't used to pushing itself so consistently. I was attempting to kick higher than I had in months, and in the process, I kicked my face and pulled my hamstring. It was minor, but I knew I needed to focus on healing instead of holding makeup parties. I was on the phone attempting to communicate this to my sales director when she reminded me, "You just started rehearsals and you already have an injury. You're 28, don't think you can dance forever."

"You told me I could do anything, why does that just apply to makeup?" I fired back.

"Come on Courtney, you need to be realistic."

I was dumbstruck. For the first time, I had solid proof that she wasn't at all interested in my happiness, she was just interested in how much profit I could turn. That could have been the moment I cut ties and saved myself a lot of trouble. That could have been the moment I stood up and bet on myself instead of some false savior of a day job. That could have been, but it wasn't, because I didn't listen closely enough. Instead of following my gut, I followed her lead, doubled down, and got serious again about eye shadow.

I continued waking up early before rehearsals to jump on coaching calls. I continued replying to text messages about how many parties I was booking and who on my team needed help selling more product. I'd roll my eyes and stay on the call. My stomach would turn whenever my phone rang. There were so many physical and mental signs and I still refused to give up because I believed the story that the answer had already been prescribed. I had already heard, and convinced myself, that keeping this sales job was the key to my creative longevity. Not my talent or my enthusiasm or the sheer fact that I *wanted* to be creative. It was this job. As much as I loved the work I was doing at this theatre, I was too stuck in the false story I had been telling myself to snap the hell out of it.

When We Lose It

Every time you step over the threshold into your creative dome, your only anchor is your intuition. As a creative, developing your intuition is what helps you decide. You decide what edit to make, what composition is right, which business deal to pursue. You decide these parameters, do your work, and then watch it succeed or fail. But what happens when we can't compute? When we don't know what the right choice is? When we don't even know what we want to communicate? How are we supposed to let intuition guide us when we feel so void of information, or so overwhelmed by information that our gut freezes up?

First we have to recognize what is happening. We have to recognize that we are losing our grip on our intuitive voice so that we can get back on track.

When you've (momentarily) lost contact with your intuition...

You go unconscious, looking for distractions both big and small.
You start worrying about the big picture instead of focusing on the specific problem in front of you.
You stop creating and focus solely on what the finished work might be one day, even though it doesn't need your attention.
You let in a lot of opinions.
You check your phone a lot.
You look at the list of things that need to get done, but don't do any of them.
You start researching other people's ways of problem solving and get frustrated that a lot of them already sound like your way.

You can be sure you've lost contact with your intuition when you are replacing it with those ideas and behaviors that do not serve the forward momentum of your work. But the beauty of intuition is that you always have it, it doesn't ever leave you - you just need to open the door and let it out.

You reconnect with your intuition by...

Staying with the difficult part of your work for ten extra minutes.
Breathing.
Asking, *What if the opposite were true?* about the answers in front of you.
Being in nature.
Making extended eye contact with another human being.
Taking a walk.
Working out.
Writing a list of possible (albeit ridiculous) solutions and trying each one of them.
Cleaning your house for the meditative benefit rather than because of the OCD.
Playing with an animal whose ability to be present probably trumps yours.
Taking a photograph.
Meditating.

There are more ways back to intuition, but the defining characteristic is that you get out of your head and back into your body. Your body knows and communicates in intricately organized and outrageously efficient ways. Your nervous system, motor skills and neural pathways all work together to guide you safely through a chaotic world. Your body is already intuitive; your mind is what shuts off communication. So, as simple as it seems, when you are feeling at a loss, the best solution is to get on your feet. Do something that makes you aware of your body, allow your mind to stop searching for the solution and watch as intuition bubbles up.

Using Intuition To Get What You Want

When you have finally connected back to that deep resonating truth we call intuition, now it's time to access its superpower.

Let's go back to the idea my acting teacher taught us about changing the energy of the room. Once you are open, vulnerable, and confident, using your intuition brings you to the next level of effectiveness. If you walk into a meeting with investors or potential collaborators, and your intuition feels bright and connected, you can perceive what your counterparts need. No, you may not know the specifics they're looking for, but you perceive how to change the energy of the room. Intuition could tell you that they are feeling tired, or goofy, or stressed. Your emotional intelligence keeps you from being socially awkward, but your intuition makes you a force. Once you intuit the energy of the room, that's when you decide how to change it. You use your intuition to lead the energy of the space. You use your strengths to transform the room into an energetic space that wasn't there before you entered. You've just made yourself the missing link.

Get it Down: Letting Your Intuition Lead

When did you make a terrible choice?

_____

_____

_____

What emotion led your decision-making?

_____

_____

_____

When did you make the best choice of your life?

_____

_____

_____

What emotion led that decision-making?

_____

_____

_____

How can you cultivate more of that emotion?

_____

_____

_____

What are you struggling to figure out right now?

_____

_____

_____

What is a problem you haven't quite solved yet? Go for a walk. Get physical. Move in some way.

_____

_____

_____

_____

_____

_____

Now come back to it and free write for five minutes. What seems to be the answer?

_____

_____

_____

Your failure is how you will make better work.

TEN:
THE
FREEDOM OF
FAILURE

There was a point in my twenties when I felt a failure. An unforgivable, hopeless, ain't-never-gonna-happen failure. In my anxious headspace, I decided I had not accomplished nearly enough and that this was an indication I would always fall just slightly short and never live out my dreams. And I was getting fat, and if not for the fact that I was already married, I would probably never get married.

I looked at every cut from an audition, every time the phone didn't ring, every month without work as the ultimate failure. As Jonathan Safran Foer puts it in one of my favorite lines from Grandpa in *Extremely Loud and Incredibly Close*, "Sometimes I can hear my bones straining under the weight of all the lives I'm not living." That's how heavily I creaked through my days.

I got through that period partially by following my sadness, but the other part was redefining my relationship to failure itself. Or maybe more accurately, my perceived failure. After I kept pushing through the same old bullshit in my head, I finally landed on what I considered one of the biggest failures of my life.

Crying On The Bathroom Floor

I have been cut from auditions left and right. I have made it to final callbacks over and over and still not heard the phone ring. I have booked a great gig and gotten a bad review. But none of these supposed failures hurt as much as the day I quit the direct sales job.

I had just come back from my summer of performing four musicals and (despite my initial instincts) sneaking in makeup parties between matinee and evening shows. I was ready to hit the next round of auditions infused with enthusiasm from the last few months, even as I sheltered the age-old anxiety of not knowing when I would book my next gig. With that anxiety and the conversation with my sales director fresh in mind, I doubled down so much on sales that I now had become a sales director myself. Meaning, I now had a full team. Meaning, I was their leader. Meaning, I had to recommit myself to their financial success to ensure my own. And since I was still equating my ability to perform with my ability to make money through sales, I got even more serious about it. To the point that I earned a car. My anxieties were so strong that I manifested a car I didn't need to show me that *Yes dammit! I'm successful! Just look at that car!*

My sales division had a retreat, and like a good leader I showed up and got my team to show up with me. We spent a few hundred dollars on a conference center for the weekend talking about hopes and dreams and making oodles of money, one moisturizer at a time. I was nodding my head yes to everything, saying the right things, and wearing the right kind of smile. My perfectionist good girl complex was in full effect, but something felt off. The weekend ended with this video montage about pursuing your dreams. There was an eagle. I think there may have been patriotic music. It was the stuff SNL sketch dreams were made of, and in any other life I would have skeptically giggled, but instead I started crying. Weirdly and uncontrollably. I was surrounded by people who were inspired by me. I had made it to sales director and earned a car quicker than anyone else on my team. I should have been crying tears of joy, I thought. I'm getting everything I wanted, I thought.

But I also knew, deep down in my bones, that I wasn't in the right place. I couldn't admit it there though, even silently to myself. Even as I watched that ridiculous eagle. I shoved the feeling back down into my gut. I didn't want to look at it. The tears were sad. The tears were fearful. I dried my eyes and said to my senior director, the one who told me to be realistic about my creative abilities, how happy I was to be part of the company and how much I could now see my dreams coming true. Fear obeyed. Instincts swallowed.

I got home that Sunday afternoon and Craig met me outside. He was so warm to me as I walked up the steps to our apartment. He took my bags, gave me a huge hug, looked in my eyes and asked how it went. He had always given me a little pushback about the sales job, so this conversation asking about the retreat surprised me. As we walked in, he put my bags down and said we needed to talk. We sat down on the couch.

He said, "Courtney, you know I believe you can do anything you want, right? *Anything* you want."
"Thanks babe, yeah I know."
"I mean it. You can do anything. Isn't that what the company tells you?"
"Uh huh."
He took a big breath. "It's time for you to quit."

I pushed him away. I scooted to the edge of the couch. He became the enemy and my body tensed up, ready to fight. Immediately. Instinctually.

"I can't do that, you know I can't do that, why would you say that?"
"You have to, we can't financially make it happen anymore," he said. Then he asked me how much debt I had.

Like many other direct selling jobs, I had to invest a lot of my own money into the product. Had I stuck it out, I might have made a profit back if I committed even more to it, but it had distracted me from my real dreams for too long. By the time I left, even though I was making about $3,000 per month, I still had close to $6,000 in debt. And the higher up in the ranks I got, the heavier the pressure to order more product became.

While I was at the retreat, Craig had spent the whole weekend researching the company. At that time, several investigative reports were working to uncover whether or not the company was in fact a pyramid scheme. He was reading personal accounts about spouses splitting up over the same kind of debt I had, and stories about how much debt people found themselves in after only a few years. He had always had a bad feeling about the business, but now he had empirical proof. On top of which (and this was truly his best point) he said,

"You're an actress. That's what you do. Not this."

I looked at him and saw the pain in his eyes. I saw the love it took to sit down someone like me, bullheaded and blind, and ask them to change course. He looked earnest and compassionate. He was resolute. He wasn't asking, he was telling. But I saw how it all came from love. I realized if anyone in the world was looking out for me, it was him, not my sales company superiors. If he thought this job was keeping me from living out my authenticity, I believed him. He knew me better than anyone else.

Shit. I was going to have to quit. I was going to have to give the car back. I was going to have to take down my stupid Facebook page. I was going to have to look for a new Day Job. But the absolute worst part of it was my team. I had led my team into this mess and now I was abandoning ship. It was too much to think about. I started choking up, my heart was racing, I thought for sure I was going to jump out of my skin. I ran into the bathroom and shut the door, dropped to the floor and started sobbing. The tears were relentless. I couldn't believe what I had done. Even more than I cared about the piles of debt I had accrued, I cared that I had potentially hurt other people in similar positions. I cared that I had convinced them this was a plausible way to make money – and to be fair, it could be, if you devoted your entire life to it. But that wasn't the pitch. The pitch was the same pitch I got: this will make it easier to follow your dreams. You'll be able to perform. Now you can be an actress forever.

Craig came in and sat with me on the floor, hugging me as I wept for letting down the women on my team and leaving them to figure it out. I was destroyed. I had never felt failure like this. This wasn't about not getting something I thought I deserved. It crushed me because I felt my character had fallen short. I had just spent the past weekend giving speeches and performing and inspiring others, and now, all of a sudden, I was admitting it was a huge lie because I hadn't paid attention to my gut. I was the most ashamed I have ever been in my entire life. I hadn't just failed, I had wiped the hell out.

After the painful conversation with my senior and her senior, during which they tried talking me out of the decision for ninety minutes, I started calling my team. I told them what I was doing and why. I told them the mistakes I had made and warned them not to make the same ones. I told them I still believed they could make it work if they made this job everything, but that if it was just to make extra money, maybe they shouldn't quit their (other) Day Job. I was completely honest, or as honest as I could be so as not to get in trouble with the company lawyers. Of the innumerable lessons I learned in that process, learning how to very badly and very publicly make mistakes and still survive them gave me more freedom than I could have ever imagined.

For a few months, I mentally beat myself up and avoided conversations when my friends asked me what had happened. I stayed locked in the apartment for far too long. The shame and guilt I had felt almost choked me to death, but I got my oxygen supply back by eventually admitting my failure out loud.

I also had to learn how to forgive myself. I looked at how easily I had been manipulated and what I did to manipulate myself and realized, as embarrassing as it was, that experience transformed me. The next time something felt off to me, I would follow my instinct. That made it easier to find the next Day Job and not fall into something that wasn't right for me. The next time I acted as if one job or gig was my salvation, I'd slow down and just be appreciative for what it was: a moment in time. That made every cut and callback easier to handle. The next time I led people, I'd make sure it was to a place I truly wanted to go.

That was the inspiration I used in developing a theatre collective with my undergraduate alumni network a month later and in beginning to write this book and in thinking about what it was I really wanted to say with my life.

So yes, I failed. Thank God.

Get Used To It

Failure is inevitable. I am not just going to say to you that failure is a lesson and so there really are no failures. No. There are real failures. Really real failures. You royally mess up an audition, you start a business that goes bankrupt, you lose the game because you miss the shot. Failure is just part of doing anything. You have to experience failure to have any idea of where you stand. Failing gives you more information, and the more information you have, the better you can articulate your vision.

The First Ten Years

If you want to be any good at your art, or your life for that matter, you have to be willing to trade in pride for humiliation. A good and humbled spirit is a resourceful one. Take the first part of the rehearsal process for example. Everyone is bumbling around, making choices that may or may not have anything to do with the context of the script, trying out accents that make it unclear if you're in Scotland or Texas. Failure upon failure. But you stick with it so you can carve away what doesn't work to find out what does.

This is true in the bigger sense too. I have made so many mistakes, stuck my foot in my mouth multiple times, bombed so many auditions and interviews. I have felt like such a failure that I was on the verge of giving up my creative life because surely there was nothing left for me. But rock bottom is kind of a cool place to be. Nowhere but up. Can't get any worse. There is something about falling down that feels safe. Failure is freedom.

Failure is freedom because you're hurt, but you're not dead.
Failure is freedom because now it's known.
Failure is freedom because you just got brand new insight.
Failure is freedom because success can feel heavy.
Failure is freedom because you're smarter.
Failure is freedom because you're tougher.
Failure is freedom because you know it'll come around again, and that's okay.

If you don't allow yourself the freedom of failure, you will not be good at doing what you do. You will be copying someone else's well-laid path, at best, or become completely stale at worst. Failure hurts, there is no doubt about it. Mistakes are painful, this is the truth. But you really can't be a creative without accepting them as milestones of your work. They are checkpoints. They are directional shifts. They are reminders. They are solutions. They are ways out and ways in. They are terrible, shitty gifts that end up being survival tools. They are necessary and abundant. To be a creative, you won't get used to the feeling that comes when you fail, but if you're any good, you will make a habit of using your failures to make better work.

Getting It Down: Failure Liberates

What was your worst failure?

_____

_____

_____

How did you know you had failed?

_____

_____

_____

What did you wish you had done differently?

_____

_____

_____

What would that successful outcome have been?

_____

_____

_____

What emotion does that bring up? How can you cultivate that now?

_____

_____

_____

MAKING IT

Our stability resides in the energy we drive into our work when no one is watching.

ELEVEN: STOP CHASING YOUR DREAMS (SO YOU CAN LIVE THEM)

When I booked my first Off-Broadway show, I wasn't even supposed to audition for it. I wandered in because I wanted to practice a new monologue for a different audition later in the week. It was a memory piece where I recalled something that had already happened, rather than a piece where I was experiencing something in the moment. Generally, this kind of material is a big no-no for auditions. These monologues are usually not exciting; there's not enough action. I knew the rules well, but I really liked this monologue and wanted to see if I could make it work anyway.

As I had found out during my *Evita* audition years earlier, the perfect costume would not necessarily set me up for success. But at this audition, I was on the other side of the spectrum. My shirt didn't fit quite right, my thick winter socks were giving me cankles through my skinny jeans, and it was snowing outside so my hair was attractively matted to the side of my face. I didn't look like a leading lady, but for better or worse, I certainly had the air of not giving too many damns about it.

The audition center was pretty quiet. The storm was keeping most people away. I didn't have an appointment, but the monitor let me dry off as much as possible and then took my headshot and resume. He said, "You can go in right away if you're ready."

I glanced over the play one more time, applied the random lipstick that was in my bag, and said, "I'm ready." I walked into the room and saw an older man and a younger woman sitting at the table. I said my hello and proceeded. Acting is a funny thing; when you're present, you don't remember anything. You don't have a sense of whether you did well or not. I don't remember anything from the audition itself, but I remember how it ended. I thought, *Okay, I can use that.*

The First Ten Years

The next day, I got an email from my agents that I had a callback. And then another one after that. And then finally I got the call that I booked the show. I was now the lead in a new Off-Broadway play, and I had walked into the initial audition thinking I was just warming up for the real deal later in the week. How can you plan for something like that? You can't. Things lined up that time. We were all in the right mood. I happened to fit the character description perfectly, although that fact alone will never guarantee anything. Maybe I changed the energy of the room by letting go of my perfectionism and letting my authentic self take the spotlight. But truthfully, who knows?

What I loved about booking that show was how much it didn't make sense. The odds were against me, but I was too present to recognize it. I have no idea why I got the role. I could ask someone, but the truth is, that gig worked out for the same reason the next one won't.

In any creative life, the only thing that can remain fixed is our intention to stay present.

We all fight against uncertainty. No matter how much as creatives we say we love change, need change, thrive in change, when change shows up we get uncomfortable. We don't like not knowing how it's all going to come down the pike. Not knowing what is going to happen next, where our next job or paycheck or break or meeting or audition will come from can be torture. We know it comes with the territory, but instead of accepting it, we start to *plan.* We articulate what we think should happen and could possibly happen and then go about obsessing over it. We turn our obsessions into a list of goals. Have you made your five-year plan? Ten-year plan? Lifetime accomplishment cheat sheet? I have, too. These are not terrible things, they're just not the whole picture. They're not very helpful in cultivating a sense of flow, happiness, joy and gratitude because they're not about the power of the present.

When we put all our eggs into that future basket, and stuff our would-be accomplishments into the perfect plan, we miss the essential element of being a creative: the ability to constantly adapt. When we decide that just one magic bullet will determine how well we're living our lives, we lose out on a million other opportunities to succeed. If we decide that we are chasing one moment where we finally get to step onto that Broadway stage or make that deal or get that investor or fill in the blank, we decide that every other part of our magnificent selves is not live-uppable to that one moment of a lifetime. We pretend that the chase has a destination instead of seeing that the chase *is* the destination. We fixate on one saving grace instead of seeing the success that's right under our nose and in our lives every day.

Don't believe me? Let's take an inventory:

What have you done that you didn't think you were ready for at the time?
What resources did you draw upon to meet the challenge?
How did you feel when you were done?
What other big accomplishments have you achieved?
Did you plan those?
Did you organize those?
Did you choose for them to happen, or was it a conglomerate of perfectly random moments that led to being in a position to hop to it when asked?

My point is: you did not strategically plan all the success you have already accomplished inch by inch, so why would you think your future success would be any different?

I was fairly ill-prepared to book an Off-Broadway show by all perfectionist control freak standards:

The audition wasn't an appointment, I just walked in off the street.
I had a weird outfit on that made no sense.
I almost didn't go because it was snowing.
It was the first time I did the monologue.
I wanted to try the monologue because, by industry standards, it wasn't a good piece.
I didn't take any time before I walked into the room to prepare or focus.

The only thing I actually put considerate thought into was the work of doing the monologue. I didn't walk into the audition center caring about certainty in my future and hoping that this would be the job to get me out of my funk, the next big thing for my resume, or a dream come true. Walking in was about surrendering to uncertainty, experimenting a little bit and relying on my resources and my sense of flow.

And, by the way, it won't work like this every time. Sometimes all the chips will fall into place, you'll be right for the part, they'll love you, and you won't get it. That doesn't carry with it a bigger meaning. That is part of the randomness of art and business. We know this, theoretically, but do we live it? Being adaptable means detaching from the meaning we make up in getting or not getting it. There is no meaning. That's not the point. The point is that despite what Anna Deavere Smith calls "unfair and chaotic realities" of being a creative, you choose adaptability, flexibility and novelty instead of stale, sad bitterness.

Consider what Oliver Burkeman writes in his book *The Antidote: Happiness for People Who Can't Stand Positive Thinking*:

"The most valuable skill of a successful entrepreneur ... isn't "vision" or "passion" or a steadfast insistence on destroying every barrier between yourself and some prize you're obsessed with. Rather, it's the ability to adopt an unconventional approach to learning: an improvisational flexibility not merely about which route to take towards some predetermined objective, but also a willingness to change the destination itself. This is a flexibility that might be squelched by rigid focus on any one goal."

Are you fixated or flexible? Are you rigid or willing? What made my one audition (of many rigid ones, I might add) good, or at least good enough to pass that first round into callbacks, was my flexibility and willingness. Not just in the flow of my immediate work, but in the trajectory of my larger body of work. I had stopped caring so much about making it so I could focus on the monologue. I detached from the final goal and trusted in the fact that I could adapt and light up when the circumstances asked that of me. *That* energy is our constant, dear friends. *That* energy is our stability. Not the accolades and articles and awards, but the energy that diffuses desperation. The energy that dissipates anxiety. The energy we drive into our work when we think no one is watching.

Get It Down: What If It All Went Away?

Being creative feels risky and uncertain, but it doesn't have to be.

What can you control?

_____

_____

_____

What can you make today?

_____

_____

_____

Who can you reach out to?

_____

_____

_____

What can you share with the world?

_____

_____

_____

What attachments do you have with your work?

_____

_____

Do you need prestige, honor, praise? Try making something really good and then don't share it. What does that feel like? Is it still worth it?

_____

_____

_____

_____

_____

_____

You "make it"
because you decide
+ "make it."

TWELVE: STANDARDS OF SUCCESS, OR, MAKING IT

One night, I was walking down 42nd Street. I was heading toward the theatre for the evening show I was starring in at the time. I had spent the day teaching and writing, and now I was about to perform in New York City. I thought, *Courtney if you don't believe that you've made it now, then you need to get out of town and do something else.* I could have easily downplayed my accomplishments – it was only *Off-*Broadway. Yes I was the lead, but was I going to be *nominated for something*? Before my head could go to that dark side, I snapped a photo of the cabs flying down Broadway. I stopped at the crosswalk and let my eyes unfocus. The colors of cars and lights and people seemed to swirl into each other, the city expanded and contracted on itself. Everything beautiful and everything ugly was on that street. It was loud and messy and lovely. If being in that moment wasn't making it, nothing was.

A Civilian's Guide To Success

If you've ever answered the cocktail party question "So what do you do?" with "I'm an actor," you're familiar with the follow ups:

Have I seen you in anything?
Have you been on Broadway?
Are you on TV?

I know those particular questions well from being an actor, but every creative faces them. Sometimes they sound like:

Where have you been published?
Is your work in a gallery?
Who's your agent?
How many followers do you have?

The First Ten Years

Where have you been featured?
How does that make you money?

It's not fair, really. Creatives get no declarative horn to blow when we've finally made it. There is no large stamp of approval that comes down on our resume and says: Real Artist, Please Pay with Real Money.

Part of the struggle is trying to describe what we're doing to other people. Civilians quantify success as visibility. And that's not really their fault, they don't understand the creative's epic journey. They don't understand that producing your own work at a small theatre in Queens is actually one of the most satisfying, badass, pro-active, life-affirming things you can do. They don't understand that playing a completely different kind of role than you're used to, in a terrible, small-budget, no-one's-gonna-see-it film is actually the mojo you need to get your butt in gear. They don't understand that heading to the streets and capturing the perfect moment with the perfect composition, movement and light is the fuel to keep your imagination on fire. Or that listening to an album by your favorite musician leads to your own musical revelation. They don't understand that the hours you sit writing, writing, writing your latest sketch late at night or early in the morning, chipping away at your plot structure or your character's relationships, are the hours that, at the end of your life, you'll look back on and say, *I really did it.* Nope, the civilian just wants to know if they can point at the TV and say, *I know him!* And truthfully, there's nothing wrong with that. Their job isn't to make your creativity retain value and integrity and honesty and depth. That's your job.

The real problem exists when we take on those awkward cocktail party questions as though they are the standards for our success. We believe that *if only* we could say, "Yes! I was in that film you paid $20 to see on

IMAX and I was paid handsomely for my Academy Award-winning work in it!" then we would somehow release the gnawing feeling that we are a fraud.

Here's the kicker: you will always feel like a fraud. No amount of money or awards will keep you from feeling like a fraud until you have decided to stop feeling like a fraud. It's a decision. It's nothing anyone else can give us. There is nothing on your resume that will definitively mean *you've made it.* Because no matter how high you climb, there is always higher, and there is always the chance of falling all the way back down.

We believe we are frauds because:
We should be making more money.
We should be working consistently.
We should have an agent.
We should have more influence.
We should be able to handpick our projects.
We should be able to buy a house.
We should be able to quit our Day Job.
We should be able to have a family.
We should be able to impress people in our hometown.
We should have won many prestigious awards.
We should not have to worry any more.

The list goes on. Do you get the point? Whether you're an actor or writer or accountant or painter or executive or baker, we each have a very personal and specific fraud checklist that we keep in the back of our heads. Oh, we may not admit to all the careless ways we value and devalue our success, but they are silent killers of dreams back there, just waiting for something good to happen so we can stifle it with the old *"that doesn't count."*

The First Ten Years

So we create this long list of "shoulds," but we never actually check any of them off. How often do we finally get something we really wanted just to downplay it when we have it in our unsatisfied little hands? I'm not talking about pretending to have a general wash of gratitude for every opportunity. We can smell that bullshit from a mile away. I'm talking about actually considering that maybe, just maybe, we *have* actually made it.

Have you ever considered that all the current circumstances of your life mean you've made it?

I'll wait.

The first time I ever really considered that was on 42nd Street at rush hour. When I stood on that corner, I could have gone in one of two directions. I could have written everything off and decided that making it looked like something else, that I wasn't quite there yet, or I could have decided that living in that exact moment embodied the success I had always been chasing. For the sake of my sanity, and to teach myself to be kind to myself when no one was watching, and because I felt really content, I chose to believe that I had made it.

As I walked toward the theatre, slower and a bit more thoughtfully, I clarified something in my head. I didn't believe I had made it because the job I booked was Off-Broadway. Instead, I had made it because, despite criticism, I fought to maintain an honesty in my process and performance that aligned with me from the inside out. Making it in that moment wasn't because of the good reviews I might get, because I had chosen not to read any of them. I had learned enough to know that during performances, they wouldn't be valuable to my growth, so I waited until we closed to read what others thought of the show. Making it depended on the simple fact that I could expose myself to the New

York City theatre world and know I would maintain the integrity of what our company had worked on, whether critics thought I was a hack, the next Meryl Streep, or forgettable. Becoming "a success" wasn't due to the potential opportunities that would propel me forward and, maybe if I was lucky, book me the next job, but the certainty I had in my abilities to do a good job, be open to feedback, and never get stuck. I made it because I decided to own it. I made it because I decided to make it.

Again, the civilian is not going to understand that. But it doesn't really matter. If you are asked the equivalent of, *Have I seen you in anything?* you can respond any which way, but if at the bottom of it you are apologetic, fidgety, and bitter that's all they will hear. If you are affirmed, grounded, and joyful, then that's all they will hear. And which one sounds more like success?

Get It Down: The New Standard

We have got to figure out how to define success for ourselves. Anna Deveare Smith wrote,

"A doctor becomes a doctor because he or she is formally given an MD. A scholar in the university is formally given a PhD, a counselor an LLD, a hairstylist a license, and so forth. We are on the fringe and we don't get such licenses."

The path to success will look different for everyone, because success is not only about accomplishments. Or rather, accomplishments are not just external benchmarks; it is an accomplishment to feel the way you want to feel every day. No one else can tell you how to do that. That's on you. So how do you want to feel?

What is the biggest accomplishment you haven't achieved yet? How would having that make you feel?

_____

_____

_____

_____

_____

_____

What has made you feel that way before?

_____

_____

_____

_____

_____

_____

What if you created that feeling right now, in this moment? What would you do? For example, if you want to feel joy, could you put on your favorite funny movie? Call a friend who always makes you laugh? Dance around the kitchen naked? There are always steps we can do immediately if we get clear about the feeling we are after.

_____

_____

_____

_____

_____

_____

Life is messiest when you are squeezing yourself into an identity that doesn't live up to your vast capabilities.

THIRTEEN: MANAGING ALL THE THINGS YOU ARE

When I was little, I would line everything up. My stuffed animals were lined up at the end of my bed, facing me so we could all see each other. I had shoe boxes full of mini "sets" (homemade doll houses with two dimensional pen-drawn pictures of sofas and coffee tables) lined up against the walls of my bedroom. Even my messes of dolls and clothing, albeit on the floor, were in a straight line. Something about this organizational structure made me feel calmer. My mom has told me that when I was a kid, the most consistent thing I said was *"Why?"* I needed to know *why* things were so I could put them in their place. I needed to understand *why* so I could compartmentalize. Lines and answers make things fit, and when things fit, the world feels safer.

So with all of this organizational mojo you'd think that a) my apartment might be cleaner than it is and b) I would struggle with having a career as unpredictable as mine. Well, no my apartment is not as organized as it should be, but yes I do sometimes struggle with being a creative. Let me get clearer: I don't struggle so much with being a creative as I do understanding how all of the different parts of me fit together. In my adulthood, I ask the same question of my career. I am an actress, a writer, a dancer, a singer, a playwright, a personal trainer, a leadership coach and I want to add documentarian and filmmaker to the list, but *why?*

When I decided that I needed a Day Job with more meaning, I started working for an up-and-coming-fitness-boutique-turned-national-brand. It was invigorating to go into work every day and contribute to the method, the writing, the training. My brain was used. My body was healthy. My heart was attached. So naturally I was worried. Was this my new career path? Was I going to quit acting like so many other almost-30-somethings who can't stand step-touching in the ensemble anymore?

Most people I talk to these days do more than one thing with their lives. Even the most successful Hollywood actors, who do not need to do anything else for money, are activists, writers; they dabble in directing. My younger, stuffed-animal-lining-up-self would have trouble with this. She wouldn't understand the correlation. She wouldn't know what to line up where.

That's because try as we might, we can't compartmentalize ourselves. Of course, we do anyway; we say that we are one thing when we are actually eight things, just because it feels more logical. It feels like we know what we're doing to define ourselves by one thing instead of eight. But the more authentic answer comes from the fact that we are whole, real people and all of our parts feed into each other. People will know us by the story we tell about ourselves, so if we have a lot of moving parts, all we need to do is get down to this baseline: *Why?*

What Do You Call Yourself?

"She was a wonder junkie. In her mind, she was a hill tribesman standing slack-jawed before the real Ishtar Gate of ancient Babylon; Dorothy catching her first glimpse of the vaulted spires of the Emerald City of Oz...she was Pocahontas sailing up the Thames estuary with London spread out before her from horizon to horizon." Carl Sagan wrote those words in his 1985 novel, *Contact*.

Wonder Junkie. It's just so good. It's concise and mesmerizing. It holds worlds in its compact string of twelve letters. You know what this person values and how far she is willing to go for it. She craves awe to the detrimental ends of obsession, to a state of consumption so unhealthy that she might find herself strung out on amazement. Two words create worlds.

The First Ten Years

The term Wonder Junkie contains a great lesson in self-definition. Naming things is important. It's a way in. We get lazy with it. Sometimes we let other people do it for us. There have been a handful of stomach-turning moments when harmless civilians have asked me if I'm an "aspiring actress." (Of course, that's not so bad as "struggling actress." In my waitressing days, I marveled at how excited tourists would get when they saw me, a real life person struggling toward her dreams by serving them Spinach and Artichoke Dip with Extra Chips. *Oh Susan, we had the best time in New York City. We saw the Empire State Building, Times Square, David Letterman, and a struggling actress. No really, she's trying to get to Broadway, just like in the movies!*)

When beginning to name ourselves, we absolutely cannot use the word aspiring. Aspiring means you're doing nothing but hoping something will happen. We creatives either do it or we don't do it. Aspiring means you're as good as dead.

Civilians' little infringements on our identities are not as bad as the ones we make ourselves. We edit away our own vitality by rejecting specificity for something more appealing to our inner stuffed animal liner-upper. We just desperately want to be liked so we make ourselves as reasonable as possible. The problem is that nothing we're doing is reasonable.

If I'm an actress and an author and a playwright and a trainer and a coach and a free creative spirit, then which easy answer do I choose when someone asks me, what do you do? I *do* all of those things. But I *am* something else entirely.

I am polycreative. A spiritual seeker. A story ninja. A meaning maker. A long form anecdotal obsessive. A polyform wordsmith. A creativity addict. An essence fiend.

Within each of these possible identities, I rattle and shake loose some assumptions I am hiding away in the back of my popularity-concerned primitive brain: the assumption that I can only be really good at one thing and I should reject everything else; the assumption that I have to fit a specific genre to be commercially viable; the assumption that I am a fraud in all of these areas because when I smash them together my personality seems messy and unkempt.

But the real hand-to-God truth is, life is messiest when we are squeezing ourselves into identities that don't live up to our vast capabilities.

We have got to vet words that will reflect our identities in that bigger sense. But this in between, this definition-less definition is the exact space where the words will show up. The more we let it breathe, the less likely we'll be suffocated by false self-advertisements, and maybe we'll find a set of words that connects with the deepest part of our self-awareness.

Cataloguing Your Loose Ends

When I left the direct sales job, I had lost money, respect for myself, and my sense of direction. I have never been lost at sea in an expanse of nothingness, but I imagined it might be like how I felt after quitting. I couldn't see the value in what I had just learned. It just felt like I had made a huge mistake.

When I performed the Off-Broadway show, it wasn't planning on transferring to Broadway. It had no forward momentum. It was simply to be opened and closed. Although I learned so much about my own process, I didn't see how it was furthering my career.

When I started at the fitness boutique, I had never really enjoyed working out before. I thought it was a great Day Job, and I loved the people I worked with, but I wasn't gauging how it would make me a better writer or performer.

It's obvious, isn't it? All of those experiences add up. Every single thing in our life is an apprenticeship, making us better for something we might not even know we are going to do yet. The terrible sales job was my apprenticeship in business. I learned how to market, how to transfer enthusiasm, how to ask for a sale. I learned the nuts and bolts of looking people in the eye and asking for money. That's a valuable thing for a creative. We don't necessarily feel good about doing that. We just want to make our art in our corner and hope someone notices. But making huge dents in the universe is a lot easier to do when you know how to go out and get funded. The Off-Broadway show taught me about my own process. It taught me how to control the making of my art, something that I hadn't actually considered up until that point. It was my apprenticeship toward authenticity. Working in the fitness industry gave me the opportunity to write, learn even more about marketing, and learn how to teach better. I learned how to get inside other people's heads in order to positively change them. It was my apprenticeship in leadership.

My point is this – no matter where we are, when we look at our circumstances as having something strategic to offer us, we can see forward a little bit better. I have clearly needed marketing skills, a stronger process, and the power to transform people even though I haven't known why yet. If instead of throwing off those apprenticeships and cataloguing them as loose ends, we see them for the gold mine they are, our direction will become much more obvious.

There is absolutely nothing that doesn't have a lesson in it. This isn't the "everything happens for a reason" speech. What I'm suggesting is that we are crafters of our own lessons. We choose what we will take out of each struggle, Day Job, or success. If we are smart, and if we want opportunities beyond what we could have previously imagined, we'll see the world in one way: we'll see everything as an apprenticeship toward our greatness.

A Quick Word On Marketing

When choosing how to market yourself, you need to recognize that the skills are different, but every story is the same. Everything is a remix, so you have to find your own specificity within that same old story. When you define the story so people can attach to it and sink their teeth in, whatever you have to sell or service or give or perform becomes tangible. When it's tangible, people will follow you.

All of this takes a minute. It is an ongoing process, and it changes much more than you would think. But if you can distill everything you do into a phrase or quality, you have refined your ability to influence. Being specific opens up opportunities, makes connections, and manifests happiness.

Marketing is a tricky term. Most of us feel a certain amount of unease in promoting our material. But that snake oil salesman you feel inside only comes out when the promotion is about you. You can promote your work in order to be useful, helpful, and to contribute to a larger conversation. Ask yourself how what you are promoting is going to benefit the public at large. Don't assume we don't want something just because it's not free. Give us credit; we consume the things we want to consume. We digest these things on the daily because we use them as identity-markers. We choose this coffee or this computer or this neighborhood or this book because it tells the world something about us. So what does your creativity communicate for us? What dots do your vision or product connect? *This* is how you market without feeling like a slime ball. You identify the need and then you fill it with your authentic talent. You become useful.

If you feel uncomfortable with what you're doing, then maybe what you're doing is focused more on checking personal markers of excellence off your list rather than figuring out how you can help the most people the most consistently. Those two actions can look a lot alike, but when you get clear about your purpose, self-promotion will be a breeze.

Get It Down: Daily Diagnosis

What do you do with your days?

_____

_____

_____

What do you do well?

_____

_____

_____

What do people thank you for?

_____

_____

_____

How do you influence the world the most?

_____

_____

_____

What words are similar or even the same from above?
This is your common denominator.

_____

Will I ever
work again?

the willingness to
consistently and

happily

deal with this question
is what makes

a creative
a professional.

FOURTEEN: WORKING ARTIST

I knew I wasn't going to book it. Well, I didn't *know* anything; we never do, but I did have a feeling that this wasn't going to be my moment. I knew I looked a little too young for the part, but as Craig supportively pointed out, approaching 30 and looking too young for certain roles is a win in and of itself. I nailed the audition – I had done *A Chorus Line* at three other theatres and knew every inch of that show. Hell, I lived that *life*. I had a great relationship with the theatre (I worked for them before on a very successful show), and the director (who happened to be a dear friend) had called me in for god's sake. It was in the bag. And I didn't book it.

When it comes to acting, that's normal. Most of the time, we don't book it. We rely on the right pieces lining up at the right time to snag the contracts we really want. Most creative endeavors in general are only commercially successful when a bunch of people agree to try and make them successful. So in our mad scramble to just get into a show, we realize that a good deal of getting in depends on seventeen different pieces fitting together in our favor.

People always ask me, how do you deal with rejection? You can't prepare to be rejected. No matter how much you steel yourself, rationalize your mind away from hope, or just acknowledge your gut instinct that it's not going to work out, the moment you find out for sure you didn't book that job still feels like a mini-beat down. Sometimes it feels like an angry linebacker shoving you under a pile of other roided-up athletes. Sometimes it feels like a petulant little kid, kicking you in your shins over and over again while you futilely yell STOOPPPPPPP. Either way, it hurts.

This particular day of rejection was also the day I was scheduled to meet with a high school student who wanted to interview me about what it's like to be a working actor in New York City. Off I went to offer some semblance of perspective from my "working actor" standpoint. I was a sweaty mess from teaching fitness all day long as I sat in the Cosi on 51st and Broadway with my third iced coffee of the day and dove into a conversation about the perils and positives of being an actor in this big, bad city.

Inevitably, because the wound was right on the surface, I told my interviewer about my fresh rejection. I told her how I was banking on this show working out, not just for the money and the Actors' Equity working weeks that would make me eligible for health insurance, but because it would have been an affirmation for me. I told her how I had set in my mind that if I could play Cassie in *A Chorus Line* as I was turning 30, that it was a sign I was on the right career path. If it had come through, it would have been an omen from the theatre gods yelling down at me, *Keep plugging away kid!* I told this sixteen-year-old how I wanted to say those lines that Cassie says because I wanted to validate all of our experiences – of holding on when it's time to hold on, of letting go when it's time to let go, and most of all, what it feels like to adjust your dreams in order to stay in the game.

I rambled and she wrote, vacuuming up all of my words and dumping them onto her notepad. I emptied all of my insecurities and understandings of the business right out into the open. But to my surprise, it didn't make me feel despondent. It didn't make me feel ashamed. It made me feel like a working actor. There I was chatting with this bright eyed, positive, hopeful, glorious, teenage girl and somehow, I felt validated by my rejection. Somehow, this rejection of work gave me some legitimate street cred. Maybe it was because through her eyes I was strong. Maybe it was her kindness and genuine curiosity in what my daily life looked like. Maybe it was because I could see her trying to figure out if she, too, could pull off this thing called a career in the theatre. Something about her kindness helped me recognize that I could be kind to myself, too. I could see my cycle of vulnerability-hope-rejection-sometimes-a-job-sometimes-not-vulnerability for what it was: longevity.

Everyone says that, for actors, auditioning is your job. That's a cute saying, and I'm not suggesting I don't believe it's your responsibility to go and get a job, but responsibility is not the only thing you've got to muster when stepping into your rightful place as a working artist. Being a working artist means dealing with your own demons a daily basis. There is no point in time when any creative breathes a sigh of relief and thinks, *I have made it. Now I'm going to put my feet up and just coast.* Even the biggest of stars and the most consistent of professionals feel the heavy dread that comes with finishing a good piece of work:

Will I ever work again?

More than the jobs on the resume, the willingness to consistently and happily deal with this question is what makes a creative a professional. We decide over and over again that we will commit to the uncertainty, the fear, the self-doubt, the competition, the stress. We decide over and over again that the desire to make something that could one day possibly be moving to a dark room full of strangers is more compelling than the fact that this state of confusion is supremely uncomfortable. We decide that to be a working artist, we have to create a life full of other things; and we decide to discard the idea that to be a creative we have to be paid for our work.

We replace it with the idea that to be a creative, we have to consistently fill ourselves up with inspiration, collect our energy from the resources around us and define ourselves not by how many stages we've worked on, but by how many times we've stayed present on those stages.

The First Ten Years

So there I was, high on caffeine, endorphins and the idea that maybe this rejection was another notch on my professional belt. Maybe this interview was the universe's way of saying, you better buck up because you're staying in it for the long haul. Because when I left and walked out onto Broadway, all I could see was potential.

Get It Down: Daily Strategy

Screw the five-year plan. What do you want to feel the most in your career? What are you doing this year to achieve that feeling?

_____

_____

_____

This month?

_____

_____

_____

This week?

_____

_____

_____

Today?

_____

_____

_____

Now?

_____

_____

_____

Don't wait. Take actionable steps. Write the email. Watch the film. Call the contact. Read the book. Go on the walk. Organize the desk. It doesn't have to be monumental. Changes happen incrementally, too. But make the move, immediately, and watch progress hustle to meet you where you are. (For more on building a no-fail plan that works 45 days at a time, visit courtneyromano.com.)

This is how we
become long-term creatives.
One small shift
at a time.
It's no more
complicated than that.

Epilogue:
THE NECESSARY EVOLUTION

There is a crossover during the first ten years where you either transition from the created to the creator or quit the business altogether. You stop waiting for life to happen to you and you move. You build your own work. You write your own story and you fight like hell to tell it.

When I was in my early twenties and just starting out, I always said, *"Oh I'm definitely not a director. I don't want to be in control, I just want someone to tell me what to do and then I'll do a great job doing it."* Now that sounds nothing like me. All I want is control, especially creative control. Whenever I'm working underneath someone else, my thoughts start running away and I start thinking that I would really love to do things my way. But I have to remember that this wasn't always the case. I evolved.

At the beginning, when I saw my friends turn to something other than acting, be it directing, or teaching, or songwriting, I used to think it was giving up. Can you believe that? I didn't think it was possible for people to not want to audition eight times a week in the hopes of one callback. I didn't think it was possible that being on Broadway was not everyone's dream. Every time I saw someone trade in that dream for something different, I didn't see it as evolution; I saw it as surrender. Silly me.

After I didn't book *A Chorus Line* that last time, despite my momentary epiphany on Broadway, I had had enough. I wasn't done with the business per se, but I was done with caring. I wasn't quitting forever, but I was just done for a minute. I needed a break. I decided to take the summer off. I didn't want to keep going into auditions for pieces that weren't inspiring to me. I didn't want to waste my time and theirs if I wasn't actually thrilled at the prospect of doing the job. If I didn't have a summer gig and my schedule was wide open, then Craig and I could plan a vacation. We could actually go somewhere and see the world. We could, ya know, have a life. In the seven years I had been in New York, this would be the first time I'd be taking a vacation.

That summer was the summer we drove up the coast of California. It was idyllic. I hope to go a great many more places in my life, but this will go down in our history as one of the best trips of our lives because it changed both of us.

One day during that trip, we stood in the middle of the desert. Nothing for miles. Well, some things: abandoned sheds to either side of our cabin, Joshua trees, insects buzzing and of course, like our host forewarned us, rattlesnakes. But when you're from New York City, even all those wild things feel like nothing.

The wind buzzed through our ears; they started ringing. We looked at each other and simultaneously asked, *do you hear that?* It was the sound of nothing. Nothing sounded like ringing, as if our ears were producing noise just to fill the void. As if the absence of sound was too much to bear and our ears had to make up something, anything, to just not be empty.

At one point I looked over at Craig and said, *I don't think New York exists here.* And it didn't. Nothing exists in the desert. It puzzles. And in so doing it points to the fact that anywhere, in any desert or city or suburb, the only thing that really exists are the thoughts we keep in our mind. I promise I wasn't smoking peyote out there. But I might as well have been.

The desert disorients in a magnificent way. It closes you off from the noisiness of human life, the traffic and checkout lines and crowded commutes. It also strips away the loudest noises of them all: the clamor of competition, drive, ambition and success. It sticks you deep in the vortex of the present moment. Dropped in with nowhere to go. It's haunting and it feels damn good.

To look for miles at vastness gives you an idea of how small you are in the context of the universe. For someone like me who had been working so hard to become someone important, this was a welcome moment of insignificance. Smallness and insignificance – two things I wasn't normally striving to maintain. But in my ever-urging mind grasping for significance, greatness, and prestige, I had been missing the point. My smallness was the pathway to my greatest authenticity.

When we got back to New York, I had fully stopped giving any shits about being on Broadway. It was still something that would be great if it happened, but it seemed arbitrary to me now. It seemed like someone else's dream, but not my own. I had switched dreams. It was exhilarating and terrifying.

The scariest part of evolution for me was the demolition of my old identity. It still felt safe back there in the past. If I wasn't going to be the woman who tries so so hard and holds all of her insecurities close to her chest and packages people's expectations in the tidy little box she learned to contain herself within back when fitting in and doing the "right thing" was the holy grail of success, then who exactly was I?

I wanted to create more. I didn't want to be in the backseat; I wanted to drive the car. I wanted to make things, finish my book, write a novel, write a play, film a documentary. Sure I still wanted to act, but in pieces that meant something. In pieces that I helped to create. I wanted my acting to be another tool in my box, not the entire box. I didn't want to sit around and wait for my turn anymore. I just wanted to take it.

The First Ten Years

Chances are you have a heavy part of yourself that holds you back from living a really creative, vibrant life, but you don't want to let it go. Preach. I get ya. It's not because we think it's okay to be held back. It's because we don't know what we'll fill our arms with once we let go of the heaviness.

So I filled my arms with an aggressive amount of truth and a sensible dose of introspection because it was something new. I didn't know if it would "work;" it may have all been for naught. But evolution doesn't come free. We pay by shredding up our egos, dissolving our control, diluting our anxieties, tearing down our expectations, muscling through our misguidance, burning every last ounce of inauthenticity and finally saying, *I don't know.*

And this is the exact spot where we can begin to create.

The blank page of *I don't know* is the only way into your gut. And your gut is the only way into your longevity. We can't keep running the rat race laid out by someone else, even if that someone else was us five years ago. To be a creative, we have to continually check in with ourselves and figure out if we're being honest.

If we can release ourselves into our own honesty, then we'll be on to something. Then we'll have some sort of currency to help us relate with the rest of the world. That honesty will get us through the uncertainty and the unpaid gigs and the rejections and the civilians asking if they've seen us in anything. That honesty is what gets us to write instead of tweet. And paint instead of taking a Day Job that withers us away. That authenticity is what gets us to influence and be influenced instead of keeping ourselves closed off. That truth gets us to expand past where we started ten years ago and grow us into the next ten.

The First Ten Years

This is how we become long-term creatives. One small shift at a time. It's no more complicated than that. We take minor steps toward our major selves every time we sit down and try to do it. It's a slow burn. Overnight success is ten years, fifteen years, lifetimes in the making. But every moment we tell the truth, we inch toward it. And every moment we tell the truth, we can go to bed at night knowing we did our work.

So from one creative to another, go do your work now. Don't read about how to do it, don't look up someone else's story, just go figure it out, one small step at a time. Just cross your threshold and make something.

We're waiting for you.

Acknowledgements

If show business has taught me anything, it's that everything, *everything*, is a collaboration. My name is on this book, but it belongs to everyone listed here. Maybe you don't normally read the acknowledgement section in a book, but I'm going to suggest that you do for this one. You know these people in your own life. Their names may be different, but the help is the same. There are people all around you who are building you up. These are mine:

I would not have understood the correct use of "effect" and "affect" if not for the sharp skills of my editor, Megan Bungeroth. Meg, your ability to track the through-line of ten intricate years of turmoil so we could cut straight to the heart was an inspiring lesson in storytelling. Your guidance has made me a better, more thoughtful, more deliberate writer. You are an artist, my friend. And effective as hell.

Match Zimmerman, your designs brought this book to another level. Your fierce attention to detail, thoughtfulness and unwavering passion for this project was infused with every stroke of the key (or brush). I'm so indebted to you for the beauty and power you added to this piece. Thank you for saying yes.

Speaking of, thanks Kara Zimmerman for lending me your husband. You are my best friend. I learned much of these lessons alongside you and, if not for our friendship, most of them would be lost to the shadows. Thanks for figuring it out with me. I love you.

And cheers to another Kara. From the inception of the book idea to the terrible drafts you read to the generous way you promote everything I'm working on, you are a dear creative cohort, Kara Griffin. Thank you for being you.

Thank you to Allie O. Koehler for always having my back, both in metaphor and in style. You were the one who got me to write again, and if not for Little Red's Well, there would be no TFTY. You are a great and loving friend. Much of my creative confidence comes from our friendship.

Kennedy Kanagawa, where do I even begin? I won the prize when you agreed to direct and edit the book trailer. The beauty, specificity and understanding you brought to the project was more than I could have asked for. You are a light.

Many thanks to Alexandra Bonetti and the whole team at The Bari Studio. Speaking of Day Job Complex, you rid me of that. The support you've given me while I wandered my way through this process was generous, loving and so compassionate. Thank you for never making me choose and always building me up.

Danny and Brigitte Ryan, you two have been creative allies for Craig and me like no other. Thank you for the ferocious support you gave me from the start, all the days and nights talking about what it takes to create art and your endless patience as I told you about yet another TED talk you really needed to watch.

Lindsey Clayton and Amber Rees of The Brave Body Project, you two are walking creative revolutions. Thank you for sharing my words and shouting my message.

Becca Schneider, you're great with a pen, old friend. Thank you for reading the second draft and still believing in this book. You are a constant support and I love you.

The First Ten Years

Benjy Shaw, you devil you. You have been a sounding board, a loving supporter and a gentle nudge every time I've needed it. Let's go make some more art together, shall we? Love you, FF.

My family has to be the most loving, scrappiest and fiercest bunch of supporters I've ever met.

Thank you Tim for being my first co-star. Beach Boys 4 Life. Also, if there is any bit of resilience and grace in my bones, I know who I got it from. I love you, big brother. Megan, you are the best big sister I never had. Thanks for the support you've always sent my way. I love you for it.

Jon, Megan and Kim, for a second set of siblings, you sure feel like blood relatives. I love you guys so much. Thank you for the oodles of high fives you relentlessly send my way whenever I'm up to something new.

Luca, Grace and Madeline, the world is a beautiful, creative place made more beautiful by your voices and visions. I can't wait to see what you make, my little loves.

Aggy, you are the best cat ever. (And now, if there were any remaining doubts, I'm officially a cat lady because I thanked my cat in the acknowledgements.)

Mom and Dad Hanson, I lucked out when I got you two for in-laws. Your love and support have been so humbling over the years. Thanks for all the mornings I have sat down to write at your kitchen table. Thanks for guiding your son with so much love and belief that he has been able to give that to me. You are, as they say, the bee's knees and

The First Ten Years

I love you.

Mom and Dad, I could write another book in thanks to you. Dad, you sat me down the day I graduated college and asked me when I was moving to New York. You took your tough love papa wings and nudged me out of the nest to create my own, even when I know that wasn't easy for you. And I love you for it. Mom, when I called you crying because I thought I might not want to "pursue my Broadway dreams anymore" and maybe you wasted your money and time and support on that dream because maybe I wanted to write a book, your first response was, "I always knew you'd be a published author. I'm proud of you who you are and you bring that to whatever you do, sweetheart. Write a book!" That kind of love has been constant from the both of you. I know enough to realize that not everyone gets that kind of generosity of spirit when they tell their parents they want to be an artist. Thank you for telling me it was more than okay to be an actress, and then a writer, and whatever the hell I wanted as long as I felt called to do it. You have been there with me on my creative path since day one. This book is a reflection of your years as much as mine. I love you without limits, forever and ever.

And Craig. You are the one who sees me at my worst and loves me anyway. You saw all the early mornings, the late nights, the grumbling, the panic, the shame, the worry, the anxiety while I wrote this book (and while I lived most of these stories) and somehow you brought out of me the rest, the gratitude, the stability, the courage, the peace and the self-love. You have stood by me when it was tough and loved me when I have been bullheaded. This book compiles only some of the moments that make you such an extraordinary human being. How I lucked out and figured out a way to stay with you forever I will never know, but I am grateful for you. Thank you. I love you.

The First Ten Years

To the reader, I've imagined you since I sat down to write this. You were my invisible best buddy, but now you are real. Maybe you are as lost as I have been and to you I say: the path will clear, keep going. Maybe you are at a crossroads in your career, life or relationship and to you I say: the path will clear, keep going. Maybe you think it's too late, there are too many obstacles, you're too old, you have too little, you can't imagine beginning again, and to you I say: the path will clear, keep going. You, dear reader, are capable of creative genius because *everyone* is capable of creative genius. It's there, locked inside, and we either choose to let it shine or snuff it out. It's time. The path will clear. Keep going.

Courtney Romano is a Barrymore Award-nominated actor and freelance writer. She lives with her husband, Craig, and their cat, Aggy, in New York City. This is her first book.

courtneyromano.com

www.ingramcontent.com/pod-product-compliance
Lightning Source LLC
Chambersburg PA
CBHW071424090426
42737CB00011B/1557